T0381098

IGNITE
YOUR POTENTIAL!

A Road Map to Discover Your Spiritual

Gifts, Find Your Purpose, and

Align to God's Divine

Design

SUSAN A. LUND

WESTBOW
PRESS®
A DIVISION OF THOMAS NELSON
& ZONDERVAN

WestBow Press books may be ordered through booksellers or by contacting:

WestBow Press
A Division of Thomas Nelson & Zondervan
1663 Liberty Drive
Bloomington, IN 47403
www.westbowpress.com
844-714-3454

ISBN: 979-8-3850-0305-1 (sc)
ISBN: 979-8-3850-0306-8 (hc)
ISBN: 979-8-3850-0304-4 (e)

Library of Congress Control Number: 2023913240

Print information available on the last page.

WestBow Press rev. date: 08/22/2023

This book is inspired by and dedicated to God, with the
intent that you as a reader will
use this road map to ignite your potential,
find your purpose, and align to God's divine design
to be all God designed you to be.

Imagine if everyone in your family,
community, small group, and church
aligned to God's divine design.
Imagine if our global church of believers
discovered their spiritual gifts,
found their purpose, and ignited their potential
to be all God designed them to be.

Together, we could fulfill the Great Commission
and the Great Commandment.

Together, we could unite and ignite the
light of Christ unto a dark world,
glorify God, and grow God's kingdom.

This is my invitation to you.

TABLE OF CONTENTS

Introduction ix
- Why I Wrote This Book xi
- Endorsements and Testimonials xv

Milestone 1: Slow Down to Speed Up 1
- Designed for Significance 2
- You Have Potential! 3
- Untapped (Unrealized) Potential 6
- Where Are You Today? 8
- Where Is Your Church? 9
- Align to God's Divine Design 11

Milestone 2: Discover Your Spiritual Gifts 15
- Context 17
- Common Barriers 20
- What Does the Bible Say? 24
- Align to God's Divine Design 29
- The Benefits of Alignment 32
- Why Are Spiritual Gifts Important? 47
- Five Consequences of Failing to Use Our Gifts 51
- Five Benefits of Discovering and Using Your
  Spiritual Gifts 59

Milestone 3: Develop Your Spiritual Gifts............................65
  •   Why God's Divine Design? 65
  •   Develop Your Spiritual Gifts—Three
      Categories of Spiritual Gifts...................................69
  •   Your Spiritual Gifts..87
  •   Awareness, Flexibility, and Fit 88
  •   How Do Spiritual Gifts Operate? 92
  •   Seven Purposes of Spiritual Gifts........................104
  •   Five Simple Steps to Develop and Use Your
      Spiritual Gifts..107

Milestone 4: Discover and Align to God's Divine Design .. 123
  •   Finding Purpose 126
  •   Lessons Learned..133

Milestone 5: Your Sweet Spot..149
  •   Ten Steps to Find Your Individual Purpose...........153

Appendix: Strategies for Churches to Use This Book.......203
  •   Roadblocks to Igniting Your Potential...................207
  •   Rules of the Road...211
  •   Outline for Small-Group Bible Study 213
  •   Sources 215
Susan A. Lund Biography..239

Introduction

Congratulations on investing in growing in your relationship with God! I am so happy you are embarking on this journey. Whether you are brand-new to the faith or have been a Christian for a long time, it is my intent to help you grow spiritually in your walk with God. If you are a leader of a church (or faith-based organization), it is my intent that you, too, will grow spiritually, grow your family, and grow God's family, the church.

If your flame has been dampened or extinguished, I believe you will be reignited to experience the fire of God from within as you apply what you read. If you have never ignited the fire of God within, I believe you will come alive as you read and apply what you learn from this book. If you are brand-new to the faith or stuck, I believe you will get unstuck and gain practical insights for growth. My experience is that when people discover their spiritual gifts, find their purpose, and align to God's amazing design for their life, something comes alive inside them.

Discovering and developing your spiritual gifts is part of God's amazing design for your life. You will never fulfill your God-given potential without discovering, developing, and aligning to God's divine design.

I love this verse in the Bible:

> "For I know the plans I have for you," declares the LORD, "plans to prosper you and not to harm you, plans to give you hope and a future." (Jeremiah 29:11 NIV)

The problem is that many people don't know God's divine design. They don't know their spiritual gifts and what the Bible says about who God says they are, or they lack an understanding of God's purpose for their life. They go to the grave with unwrapped gifts, buried talents, unrealized dreams, and unrealized potential; as a result, they miss out on the great adventure and joy of being all God designed them to be. They settle for less when they were designed for more.

When people discover their spiritual gifts, find their purpose, and uncover God's divine design for their life, they recognize that they are part of God's epic story, designed to glorify God and make a difference in the lives of others. They ignite their God-given potential and either start or continue on their journey to be all God designed them to be. They come alive!

> For as in Adam all die, so in Christ all will be made alive. (1 Corinthians 15:22 NIV)

The closer we become to God, the more passionate we become. I have taught courses at our church and coached hundreds of leaders. I have observed firsthand that when people discover their spiritual gifts, find their purpose, and align to God's divine design for their life, they experience the joy of being a vessel for God.

There are benefits of aligning to God's divine design to ignite your potential and be all God designed you to be!

Here is what you can expect from reading this book:

Learn how to …

- gain clarity and find your purpose
- discover and develop your spiritual gifts
- align to God's amazing design
- experience the joy of glorifying God
- ignite the light of Christ in you
- live a life of significance serving others

- ignite your God-given potential to advance God's kingdom
- grow yourself and grow God's church
- be all God designed you to be

As a church ...

- inspire, equip, and empower people to ignite their God-given potential
- common framework to mobilize your team to ignite the light of Christ
- unite the body of Christ, His church
- gain a renewed sense of passion
- increase engagement
- reduce attrition
- increase spiritual maturity
- grow, strengthening the body of Christ
- glorify God and advance His kingdom
- alignment to God's divine design
- be all God designed His church to be

Why I Wrote This Book

I felt compelled to write this book because God inspired me to. Why? Because so many people, including Christians, struggle because they don't know God's divine design for their life. They don't know they have been given spiritual gifts, what this means, or how to develop them. Many don't know their purpose and lack a plan to fulfill their God-given potential. When this happens, people extinguish their potential instead of igniting it. When individuals, families, and believers extinguish their potential, they become impotent as a body of believers.

When I first heard someone say they lacked purpose, didn't know their spiritual gifts, and didn't have a plan to use their gifts, it made my heart ache. Where does this occur? In the church, the workplace, and our daily lives. The lack of understanding and applying what the Bible says about spiritual gifts is one of the greatest gaps in the church today. As for the workplace and our daily lives, many people lack workplace and life satisfaction or have lack of clarity on what they want to do when they grow up. For the next generation, this is amplified into a lack of purpose—going to college, yet not knowing what they want to do in life. It also shows up in the workplace as low engagement. For years, the Gallup organization has shared that nearly 75 percent of the workforce is not engaged, costing organizations millions of dollars in attrition, low productivity, and dissatisfied employees. How much does it cost? Employees who are not engaged or who are actively disengaged cost the world $7.8 trillion in lost productivity, according to Gallup's State of the Global Workplace: 2022 Report. That's equal to 11 percent of global GDP. This lack of work and life satisfaction spills over into churches; disengaged members often leave the church.

God places a burden upon our hearts—to help His people. After four years of prayer, study, and teaching this content at church, God guided me to write this book to be used in small groups, education classes and leadership teams to help people navigate around these challenges.

God also placed a desire in my heart in 2017 to grow His kingdom, His family of believers, God's church. As a businessperson, I thought, *How am I supposed to do that? Who, me? I am not a pastor; I am a businessperson.* After studying God's Word and praying, I realized that God doesn't call the equipped; rather, God equips the called. Therefore, I knew I just needed to trust God. After all, God is a God of the "how and when." In other words, we don't have to know the how and when to get started. We just need to start. I later realized that God planted the seed of discovering and developing my spiritual gifts, purpose, and God's divine design in me twenty-eight years ago and

> *God is a God of the "how and when." In other words, we don't have to know the how and when to get started. We just need to start.*

that He had led me to help others do the same before He led me to write this book. It's amazing how God guides us when we seek Him. Thankfully, God doesn't give us the entire picture all at once. If He did, it might be overwhelming!

When individuals don't ignite their God-given potential, they experience challenges:

- miss out on God's purpose and plan for your life
- unrealized potential, settling for mediocrity, not living up to your potential
- lack focus, direction, and meaning in life
- busy but not productive
- lack of confidence and struggle with decision-making
- disengaged and apathetic, fatigued, discouraged, fearful, lack of hope, feeling of defeat
- don't know your gifts, what they mean, or what the Bible says about spiritual gifts
- don't embrace your spiritual gifts or understand how to develop them
- miss out on understanding God's divine design and what it means
- extinguish their potential, bury their dreams and talents, and become spiritually impotent

When churches don't ignite their God-given potential, they experience challenges. Individual challenges above become church challenges that lead to the following:

- attrition and/or lack of loyalty, thus people leave
- plateau or decline in growth of the church; "87% of churches are stagnant or declining," according to Ray Johnston, Bayside Church senior pastor
- unrealized potential and low engagement
- 50 percent of pastors are discouraged and want to leave their job (according to recent statistics)

- spiritually immature believers with no plan to mature spiritually
- lack of teaching on how to personally discover, develop, and align to God's divine design
- lack of alignment to be all God designed you to be
- struggle to find enough volunteers to fulfill the ministry of God
- multiple unmet needs in the church and community
- becoming spiritually impotent

Bottom line, many individuals and churches are not realizing their potential to be all God designed them to be. As a result, they are not growing like they could be. They are missing out on the rewards and blessings of God. They are ignorant of their spiritual gifts, unsure how to use them to grow God's kingdom, and lack clarity of their purpose. They feel powerless instead of powerful vessels for God. They are missing out on living by God's divine design.

It doesn't have to be that way. If you are experiencing any of these challenges, know this: you can overcome them by applying what God reveals to you and what you learn in this book. I believe leaders are brokers of potential. Every person has an opportunity to lead and steward their life to ignite their God-given potential.

If you are a leader of a church or organization, I believe you can overcome these challenges. You can make a difference in your church and your organization. If you are a people leader, you can implement this book and these principles in your church. I believe God's church is at a critical juncture, especially as the world gets darker. We, as a church, need to pivot quickly to ignite our God-given potential to be powerful vessels for God and be the light of Christ and fulfill God's vision and mission in a dark world. God has placed a burden in my heart to help you and your church grow, navigate around these challenges, and be all God designed you to be.

Imagine if everyone in your church and God's church was aligned to God's divine design and fired up to do the work of God! We could ignite our God-given potential to be all God designed us to be! We would become an army for God at a time when we need to be united and strong. I can't think of a better time to be united and powerful vessels for God, to be all God designed us to be. Of all the times in history to strengthen and grow God's church, the time is now.

What challenges are you facing? What challenges is your church facing?

Don't wait any longer. If nothing changes, nothing changes. Don't cheat yourself out of the rewards God wants to give you! Ignite your God-given potential and be all God designed you to be. Regardless of where you are, you were made for more! So is your church!

Refer to appendix at the back of this book to select the best option to ignite your potential.

Endorsements and Testimonials

"Susan Lund invites us to shape our leadership and involvement to fit our particular spiritual gifts to our unique ministry context. I have known Susan for 20 years as her pastor, and she is a leader who has a heart to glorify God and grow the church of Jesus Christ. This is a wonderful, user-friendly guide to help all of us realize our potential, develop it, maintain our growth, and ultimately finish well!"

Ken Geis, Pastor

"My #1 takeaway from reading this book! We were uniquely designed by God, for God. Our design influences our entire being-it is not exclusive to work in the church-it makes us who we are in our home, work, relationship, and church life. When we are in alignment with our design, we have joy and purpose which honors God and allows us to follow the path he intended for us. I would highly recommend this book to anyone who wants to be successful and grow spiritually."

Beth Geurink

The following is feedback from people who participated in a small-group study.

What was most beneficial about our time together?

- Teaching. Everything. I am learning so much about my spiritual gifts.
- This was a game changer for me. It sets the course for my future. Thank you so much!
- Getting to know others in our group and share our testimonies.
- I loved the outlines and homework. Hearing stories from participants.
- It is so clear that God rescues us all in our time of need. He is our source.
- I learned so much about my spiritual gifts and how I can include and use them in my daily life. I gained clarity on my purpose.
- I loved to hear other people's experiences and perspectives about spiritual gifts.
- Susan shared her own experiences and how she overcame her challenges, which makes her relatable. Susan was always so encouraging, open, and continued to give us scripture and reinforce that God is for us, we can defeat the enemy and tell him to flee.
- I like having time each week to look forward and liked our small-group Bible study. This Bible study allowed me to do a lot of self-discovery and begin the process of finding out what my calling is and figure out in what way I can serve the Lord and help others.
- Such a wonderful time! There were times where I wasn't fully there and almost didn't attend, but then I would be so glad I did because I learned something new every time.
- This Bible study is the first seed in the process of finding what to do with the next fifty years of my life. In the first fifty years, I dedicated my life to being a daughter, a student, a wife, a mom, and a social worker. I feel like in the next

fifty years, I will be a Christian first and find ways to serve people outside of my family/friends.

- Each week was planned and engaging. I loved how Susan engaged everyone.
- The tools and teaching were great.
- For the first time, I was able to make a list of the dreams God has placed in my heart!

This small group study helped me to …

- Learn the in-depth details about spiritual gifts and use my gifts.
- Because of this teaching, I am now considering ways I can use my difficult life events to support and serve others in similar situations (divorce, abuse, violence, remarriage, integration of blended families).
- Listen for God's Word and be open to what He is trying to tell me.
- Continue to spend time with God, ask Him to reveal to me His plan and purpose for me and how I can be part of his plan to bless others and use my spiritual gifts. I will find ways to serve others.
- I loved all the nights of our small-group Bible study. The last night of our study was so effective in exploring what God's calling may be for me. Thank you for your heart. Thank you for appreciating my beautiful gifts.
- It was such a transformative and powerful experience. Thank you so much! I even shared it with my husband and plan to share with friends too.
- Susan, thank you so much for your Christ-centered guidance, your willingness to be vulnerable about your own personal experiences, and for giving so much time and effort to teaching us. I will be watching for your next class!
- Susan always had an organized plan and made the time we spent together well worth it.
- Susan's enthusiasm for teaching about the Lord is contagious and inspiring.

MILESTONE

Slow Down to Speed Up

It sounds counterintuitive, but to speed up, we need to slow down. I remember when I started running with marathon runners. Every morning we ran, they would say, "Slow down!" I didn't like to run slowly, but as I increased my distance from running three miles to six miles and then ten miles before work, I realized why they said to slow down. Long distances require endurance, and endurance is developed by slowing down to speed up. The same applies in life. As we run our race with endurance, it's beneficial to slow down to speed up.

I am inviting you to slow down, align around some common definitions, and assess how much potential you are actually using as you embark upon this journey to be all God designed you to be. This will help you run your race with endurance and ignite your potential! Let's start with your design.

Who designed you? God designed you. To know your design, you need to know your designer.

> This is what the Lord says—he who made you, who
> formed you in the womb, and who will help you: Do
> not be afraid, Jacob, my servant, Jeshurun, whom
> I have chosen. (Isaiah 44:2 NIV)

God designed everything in the world and spoke it into existence. Genesis 1 states that on the
sixth day, God created man and made man in His image to be fruitful and multiply.

The Bible tells us that it was God who created us. God is our designer.

> Then the LORD God formed a man from the dust
> of the ground and breathed into his nostrils the
> breath of life, and the man became a living being.
> (Genesis 2:7 NIV)

Since God designed you, discovering God's design, developing, and aligning to God's divine design is essential to ignite your God-given potential. We can't do this on our own but via a relationship with God the Father, Jesus our Savior, and the Holy Spirit as our guide.

Designed for Significance

As we get started on this journey, I want you to know that you were designed for significance. God has designed you to make a difference in this world, to bless others and do His work. Significance is all about doing the work of God, being part of His epic story from beginning to end. You were designed for so much more than this time here on earth. You were designed to spend eternity with God.

What's the difference between success and significance? Success is when you succeed as an individual and claim the reward. Significance is when you add value to the lives of others for the glory of God. Significance is about doing what God designed us to do. God didn't design you and me for just success; He designed us for so much more—significance. Significance is all about serving. We were designed to serve God and help others.

I learned this early on in my career. I started off in sales, and when I succeeded and won awards, my manager asked me to train, coach, and mentor the new hires. When I did, I found that they had great success. While I wanted to win awards (and did), it was a lot more fun to help others succeed. As a Christian, my heart was postured to glorify God and to be a vessel to bless others with what He blessed me with. Once you taste significance, success no longer satisfies. You see, it is so much more fun to help others succeed and glorify God than to live for oneself. Significance is all about serving. God designed us to serve! When you step into God's amazing, divine design for your life, you experience the great joy of serving others and glorifying God. The question is, how do you discover your gifts, purpose, and God's divine design? This book provides a road map for you to do just that!

You Have Potential!

If you asked me what I would say to the next generation, I would say, "You have potential! Align to God's divine design to ignite it and be all God designed you to be! I want you to know God has designed you for so much more than you are today. He has placed a treasure inside of you." The Bible tells us that you are God's workmanship.

> For we are His workmanship, created in Christ Jesus for good works, which God prepared beforehand that we should walk in them. (Ephesians 2:10 NKJV)

That means we are created by God for God. The word *workmanship* means masterpiece. God's greatest masterpiece of creation is each of us. God created you and me to do His good works. He created you and me to make a difference in the lives of others. He designed you to be unique, to bless others with what He has given you, and to do the work of God while you are on this side of heaven.

We were designed with an innate need to ignite our God-given potential to glorify God. If we don't, we miss out on being all God designed us to be.

What is potential anyway? Potential is the capacity to become more, to develop into more tomorrow than you are today. Since God gives us everything we have, we are talking about igniting your God-given potential and becoming all God designed you to be according to His plan and purpose.

If you don't know God's divine design and purpose for your life, you will miss out on all God designed you to be. When this happens, people extinguish their potential instead of igniting it.

What's the connection to spiritual gifts? Spiritual gifts and your God-given design reveal your purpose.

Individuals, teams, and churches are not realizing their full potential without understanding what the Bible says about spiritual gifts. If they don't gain this biblical understanding, they won't be able to be all God designed them to be. In 1 Corinthians 12:1 (NIV), Paul writes, "Now about the gifts of the Spirit, brothers and sisters, I do not want you to be uninformed."

If you are a people leader, your job is not only to ignite your potential but also to help others ignite their God-given potential. It doesn't matter where you lead; this is what an effective leader does. If you want to be an effective leader in your family, in the workplace, in your community, or in your church, your job is to ignite your God-given potential and the potential of others.

The Bible says that leaders are brokers of potential. In Romans 12:6–8, Paul describes seven gifts, distributed to different members in the body of Christ. As a successful leader, he recognizes his role as a broker of gifts, talents, and resources. He urges everyone to discover, develop, and distribute their gifts. What does he mean by *distribute*? To use one's spiritual gifts to serve others and glorify God. Successful leaders recognize that they are stewards of their own gifts, talents, and abilities and help people become more to realize, ignite, and maximize their potential.

If you are a leader of people at your church or organization, know this: successful leaders recognize that people are their greatest asset. They see people as opportunities to develop, not as problems. The sad reality is that some leaders avoid people or see them as problems. It doesn't have to be that way. God sees people's potential and wants us to steward it well to glorify God.

I do a lot of leadership training, and leaders will often ask me, "Do you think I can be a good leader?" I share with them the criteria to be a good leader and ask them, "Do you love people?" To be a great leader, one needs to love people and develop a heart to serve people.

As a leader, you are a broker of potential for everyone on your team. If you don't have a plan to help others realize, ignite, and maximize the potential of those who work with you and attend your church, what can you do? This book can be used as a tool to inspire, equip, and empower individuals, teams, and your church to ignite your potential and be all God designed you to be.

A leader's job is to inspire, equip, and empower people to ignite and maximize their potential. Who was the best model of this? Jesus. Jesus inspired, equipped, and empowered us to reach our potential with His

> *I love what Steven Covey says: "Leadership is communicating to people their worth and potential, so they clearly see it in themselves."*

death and resurrection so we could receive salvation, spend eternity with God, and be free from sin. God placed the Holy Spirit in us to guide us and be our advocate and helper. Without Jesus, we would not be able to achieve our God-given potential.

One thing we have in common is that people want to be challenged to grow and become more. What happens if you don't ignite your potential and help others do the same? People leave, or, even worse, they become disengaged but stay in your church. This prevents the church from being all God designed it to be. God's church is made up of believers, and we are to be the light to the world. We are to be Christlike in all we think, say, and do.

When people don't know their spiritual gifts, their purpose, and God's plan for their life to be all God designed them to be, they extinguish their potential and the potential of God's church.

God sees your potential! He created you with potential. He knows who you can become as an individual, a team, and a church. To ignite and realize your potential, it is essential to look at God's Word, which is the truth. Throughout this book, we will review God's Word to build a foundation of truth.

Untapped (Unrealized) Potential

Did you know that God places riches and a treasure inside of you to reveal His glory, not yours? God wants to you to experience the fullness of your God-given potential. God wants you, your family, and your church to become all He designed it to be.

Many people are full of unrealized potential, unfulfilled dreams, unwrapped gifts, undeveloped talent, unrealized potential, under-utilized energy, and unused success, which leads to an unfilled life. Some people even bury their gifts and never realize all God designed them to be. Some people deny that they have potential or gifts. I remember talking to a woman who asked what I was doing. I told her I was teaching a spiritual gift course that evening. She said, "I don't have any gifts." My heart ached to think that she was going through life without discovering, developing, and using her gifts to be all God designed her to be. Another said, "I don't like my gifts." She doubted that her gifts were valuable. I want you to know that you are valuable to God. You are God's masterpiece. God designed you with at least one spiritual gift! You were designed by God to make a difference in the lives of others! You were made for more!

Others doubt that they could ever achieve the dreams God placed in their heart or fear going after them. You may have heard someone say, "He who buries his talent is making a grave mistake." God designed us to be involved with His work. To inspire and equip us by His Holy Spirit, He freely distributes gifts to all who are saved. He not only wants us to know our spiritual gifts, but He expects us to grow in them each day and distribute them to bless others. Your spiritual gifts are part of God's divine design for your life. They are linked to your purpose, which will discuss in the next chapter.

> But to each one of us grace was given according to the measure of Christ's gift. (Ephesians 4:7 NKJV)

> To each is given the manifestation of the Spirit for the common good. (1 Corinthians 12:7 NIV)

> But one and the same Spirit works all these things, distributing to each one individually as He wills. (1 Corinthians 12:11 NKJV)

This means that every Christian has a spiritual gift to discover, develop, and distribute or use to bless others and glorify God. Every Christian can experience the wonder and joy of blessing others and being a vessel for God daily.

> *Every Christian can experience the wonder and joy of blessing others and being a vessel for God daily.*

I hope that by reading this, you will discover, develop, and align to your God-given design so you can ignite your God-given potential and be all God designed you to be.

Complete the simple assessment below to identify how much of your potential you are using today and what's holding you back from becoming all God designed you to be. If you are a leader of a church or a faith-based organization, I encourage you to take both the individual and organizational assessments.

Where Are You Today?

Spiritual Gift and Potential Assessment
What percentage of your God-given potential are you using?
Answer each question with a 1 for no or a 2 for yes.

Discover My Spiritual Gifts and Align to God's Divine Design	No (1)	Yes (2)
I know what spiritual gift(s) are.		
I know what the Bible teaches about spiritual gifts.		
I know my spiritual gifts.		
I have taken an assessment to discover my spiritual gifts.		
I have listed my spiritual gifts and what they mean in writing.		
I know my family's spiritual gifts (my spouse, my children, my siblings, and/or my parents).		
I know God's purpose for my spiritual gifts.		
Total		

Develop My Spiritual Gifts and Align to God's Divine Design	No (1)	Yes (2)
I have a plan to develop my spiritual gifts.		
I consistently use my spiritual gifts with God's family of believers.		
I am encouraging my family to develop their spiritual gifts (my spouse, my children, my siblings, and/or my parents).		
I have goals and action plans to develop and use my gifts to serve others.		
I intentionally and consistently use my spiritual gifts to serve others at home, in my community, and/or in the workplace.		
I consistently experience joy using my gifts to serve others.		
Total		

I Am Aligned to Living God's Divine Design	No (1)	Yes (2)
I know God's purposes for my life.		
I know my purpose for my life.		
I know God's divine design and why it's important.		

My work inside or outside the home is aligned with God's divine design. As a result, I enjoy or love what I do. I am fully alive in Christ!		
I know the dream God placed in my heart and am pursuing it.		
I have a plan to intentionally live my life in alignment with God's divine design and bless others, honoring God with my life.		
I am intentionally becoming all God designed me to be, using what God gave me to consistently serve others and advance God's kingdom.		
Total		

Add up your three totals. If you score under forty, you have an opportunity to ignite your potential and be all God designed you to be. Align to God's divine design! Get started today and enroll in a spiritual gift course at your church or use this book with your small group. If you don't have a small group, you can start one or join one.

Where Is Your Church?

Spiritual Gift and Potential Organization Assessment
What percentage of your God-given potential are you using?
Answer each question with a 1 for no or a 2 for yes.

Discover Our Spiritual Gifts	No (1)	Yes (2)
My organization helps all new members discover their spiritual gifts.		
All the members of my church or organization know their gifts.		
Our leadership team has taken an assessment to discover our spiritual gifts.		
We have one consistent, written definition of spiritual gifts and what they mean and have communicated this to everyone in our organization.		
I know my congregation or organization's spiritual gifts, including which are dominant and which are less dominant.		
My congregation or organization knows God's purpose for spiritual gifts.		
Our leadership team knows God's purpose for our organization's spiritual gifts.		
Total		

Our Leadership Team Develops and Uses Our Spiritual Gifts	No (1)	Yes (2)
Our organization trains individuals to create a plan to develop spiritual gifts.		

	No (1)	Yes (2)
Our leadership team consistently uses their spiritual gifts with God's family.		
Our leadership team encourages everyone in our organization to develop their spiritual gifts to build up others, improve (edify) God's church, and serve others.		
Our leadership team has written goals and action plans to develop and use their spiritual gifts to serve others.		
Our leadership team intentionally and consistently uses our spiritual gifts to serve others in our organization, community, and/or workplace.		
Our leadership team consistently experiences joy using their gifts to serve others.		
Total		

I Am Aligned to Living God's Divine Design	No (1)	Yes (2)
Our church trains and helps everyone know God's purposes for their lives.		
As a leadership team, we know God's purposes for our lives and help others know them as well.		
We train people to discover their spiritual gifts, passions, abilities, and God's divine design and why it is important.		
As leaders, we all know God's divine design and one another's spiritual gifts		
Our work is aligned with God's divine design. We experience joy at work.		
Our church helps people know and pursue the dream God places in their hearts.		
We, as a leadership team, have a plan to intentionally live our lives by God's divine design and bless others with what we have been blessed with.		
As leaders, we are intentionally helping people at our church/organization become all God designed them to be and consistently serving others.		
Total		

Add up your answers. If you score under forty, your leadership team has an opportunity to ignite your potential and be all God designed your church to be. Get started today and enroll your people in a spiritual gift course at your church or use this book with your small groups.

Align to God's Divine Design

1. What percentage of your God-given potential are you using today?

2. What do you know about God's divine design for your life?

3. What unrealized dreams are still inside of you that God wants to release?

4. What buried talents are still inside of you?

5. What percentage do you want to be using in ninety days?

Now that you know your score and where you want to be, identify the areas where you scored the highest and build upon those. Then identify the areas where you scored the lowest and focus on strengthening those areas. I also encourage you to ask yourself, "What's preventing me from becoming all God designed me to be?" If you don't know the answer, you can pray for God to reveal it to you. At the end of this book, I encourage you to retake the assessment to find out where you are.

What is the opposite of ignite? Extinguish! What, specifically, happens when we extinguish our potential? It opens the door to defeat, regret, and impotence for God's kingdom. What does defeat sound like? "I don't have potential. I don't have gifts." When one says that, they deny God in them. It dampens, if not extinguishes, their God-given potential.

That not only opens the door to defeat; it oppresses and defeats God's masterpiece, you. Don't give Satan an open door to defeat. Instead, partner with God; get in agreement with God to use the gifts He has given you to bless others for His glory. The enemy, Satan, doesn't want you to read this book, ignite your God-given potential, or know God's divine design for your life. In fact, the enemy will try to distract you and tell you that you are not worth it. Don't believe those lies, which will extinguish your potential. Keep your eyes focused on Jesus and ignite your God-given potential!

> For from him and through him and for him are all things. To him be the glory forever! Amen. (Romans 11:36 NIV)

> The LORD works out everything to its proper end. (Proverbs 16:4 NIV)

The closer you come to God, the more ignited and alive you will become! Why? God is light and truth, and in light and truth, you have life! Because God is life!

> Those who look to him are radiant; their faces are never covered with shame. (Psalm 34:5 NIV)

Doing the work of God for the glory of God brings us the greatest joy we can ever experience. God's glory is the expression of His goodness and all His other intrinsic, eternal qualities. The greatest joy is being a channel for God's grace and love, serving others for the glory of God.

I believe our highest honor is to seek to know God more, to walk with God, and to live for God's glory. As we learn God's Word, God's will, and God's design for our lives, we can align and use what we have been given to live for God's glory. Our spiritual gifts, talents, abilities, purpose, and everything God gave us can be used for God's glory.

> being confident of this, that he who began a good
> work in you will carry it on to completion until the
> day of Christ Jesus. (Philippians 1:6 NIV)

As we place our trust in God, seek God, and obey Him, He draws out our potential. As we know God more, the Holy Spirit ignites and illuminates the Word of God in us to renew and transform our thinking, changing our desires to align with God's will and God's amazing design so we can be all God designed us to be. The Holy Spirit ignites our potential because of what God did for us by sending His only Son, Jesus, to die on the cross so we may be forgiven of our sins, have eternal life, and live victoriously. We can't do this without the Holy Spirit. We are created with an inner need to be with God, to belong to God's family, and to become all God designed us to be. God equips us with everything we need to be all He designed us to be. Applying what you learn in this book will help you live to the fullness of your God-given potential.

Discovery and Application Questions: Align to God's Divine Design and Ignite Your Potential!

1. What did I learn?

2. What does the Holy Spirit want me to do today?

3. What can I apply or do to align to God's divine order and design?

Don't extinguish your potential! Take action to ignite your God-given potential, serve others, and be all God designed you to be.

MILESTONE

Discover Your Spiritual Gifts

Let's get started discovering your spiritual gifts. Doing so will also help you understand God's purpose for your life. I am excited about what God is going to teach you as you begin this journey. I believe that you are reading this for a reason and that God has a plan for you today. As we get started, let's pray.

Prayer:

"Lord, thank You so much for giving me a spiritual gift(s) and purpose. As I embark upon this journey with a community of believers, I come to You with a hungry heart to know You better and to love You more. Help me to discover and develop my spiritual gifts and to use them to glorify You. Reveal to me what You want me to know, say, and do with what I learn. Holy Spirit, give me eyes to see what You want me to see, ears to hear, and an open heart to receive what You want to impart in me. In Jesus's name, I pray. Amen."

Prayer is very important. It's your conversation with God. This prayer is something you can use going forward if you'd like. Why is that important? Sometimes people don't hear God because they have not asked God to speak to them or learned how to listen to God. When we ask the Holy Spirit to reveal to us, to open our eyes, ears, and hearts, God will speak to us. Believe and expect to hear God speak to you. You will be amazed at what God reveals to you. How might God speak to you? God's primary way of speaking to us is via His Word, the Bible. God's revelation can come through an insight, an idea, a thought, an impression, a word, a picture, a prompting to act out of love, an inner peace or knowing, nature, or others. God has spoken to me through all of these methods.

What is the difference between information and revelation? Information doesn't change us, but revelation does. What is revelation? Revelation is information illuminated by the Spirit of God. It renews our mind and gives us insight, an awakening that we didn't have before. This helps us see things from God's perspective, to know God more, and to grow spiritually.

I believe God will speak to you as you read this book. I believe God will open your heart and eyes to see what it is He wants to reveal to you during our time together. I know the Lord has a good plan for you to grow in your understanding and use of your spiritual gifts, purpose, and unique design to honor God and to advance His kingdom. The more you seek to know God and fill yourself with the Word of God, the more you will hear God.

I believe that not only will you hear God but that something will come alive inside of you. I also believe you will be able to use this book in your small group, as a leadership team at church, and in your organization to help others know God more and grow in their relationship with God. I have used this information in small groups and with leaders, pastors, and individuals one-on-one, and it has been amazing to experience how God has ignited the potential in others! All glory goes to God. I am simply a vessel.

Context

More than twenty-eight years ago, God led me to discover my spiritual gifts. I remember how excited I was the day I discovered my spiritual gifts of leadership, teaching, and faith. Later, He revealed how my purpose was linked to my gifts. Once I learned my gifts, I asked three questions:

1. If these are my gifts, what do they mean?
2. How do I develop them?
3. How do I use them to add value to the lives of others and glorify God?

As you can imagine, that sent me on a journey that has included many conversations around spiritual gifts, especially during the last ten years.

The biggest ah-ha moment for me was when nearly everyone I talked with was in one of three categories:

Category 1: They didn't know their spiritual gifts and what they meant. Almost 90 percent of people fell into this category. Nearly 30 percent didn't think they had spiritual gifts at all.

Category 2: Some knew their gifts yet lacked a plan to develop them.

Category 3: They knew their gifts yet didn't know what the Bible teaches about spiritual gifts or how they are linked to their purpose.

From talking with hundreds of Christians about spiritual gifts, my experience is that there is a big gap in all three categories. While many have heard about spiritual gifts, they have not been able to accurately apply what they have heard or what the Bible teaches on the subject to their lives. C. Peter Wagner, in his book *Discover Your Spiritual Gifts*, references similar research done by George Barna, who found that a remarkable number of born-again

Susan A. Lund

Christians who have heard of spiritual gifts do not think they themselves have any spiritual gifts. In 1995, the percentage of born-again adults who did not think they had a spiritual gift was 4 percent. But by 2000 that number had risen to 21 percent.

Personally, I find this very alarming! If this trend continues, which I believe it has, we will have a spiritually immature church body that will become impotent. God's church becomes impotent and less effective in fulfilling God's purpose when they do not know and apply what the Bible says about spiritual gifts, abilities, talents, and purpose.

> *Personally, I find this very alarming! If this trend continues, which I believe it has, we will have a spiritually immature church body that will become impotent.*

Individuals miss out on living in alignment with God's divine design and lack clarity on their purpose, which also creates impotence. It doesn't have to be this way! I believe we need to align to God's divine design and reverse this trend. I know from teaching, leading small groups at church, and working with leaders, we can reverse this trend.

Discovery and Application Questions: Align to God's Divine Design and Ignite Your Potential!

1. Where are you: category 1, 2, or 3?

2. Where is your church?

3. What did God reveal to you?

4. Where do you want to be in ninety days?

Don't extinguish your potential! Take action to ignite your God-given potential, serve others, and be all God designed you to be.

Common Barriers

As I worked with individuals, they asked me questions like "Why didn't my pastor teach us this? Why doesn't our church teach spiritual gifts?" I didn't have an answer, so I prayed, read the Bible, and continued to talk to pastors to find out why they didn't teach people how to discover, develop, and use their spiritual gifts to serve and bless others.

I learned that this is a multifaceted problem:

1. While many churches are focused on salvation, not all have a pathway to spiritual growth, discipleship, and stewardship. This is critical to develop a strong church body and do the work of God. After all, if we are called to fulfill the Great Commission and the Great Commandment, we need a strong church body.
2. Not all leaders view their people as opportunities to develop or value teaching enough to invest in them. As a result, they don't allocate resources to create an education plan, strategy, curriculum, and process for spiritual growth.
3. Not all pastors know what the Bible says about spiritual gifts or have a process at their church to teach people how to develop and use them for God's glory.
4. Some churches streamline their services and don't make room for spiritual gifts.
5. Not all Christians know what spiritual gifts are or why they are important to fulfilling God's vision and mission for His church.

I believe that aligning to God's divine design and igniting your God-given potential is a shared responsibility between leaders and individuals. As such, I don't want you to wait for your leaders to teach you this. As believers, we have a responsibility to seek to know God more every day, to study His Word, and to apply His Word.

You can learn what I have learned by developing an intimate relationship with God, seeking God's will, studying His Word, reading this book, and applying what you learn.

I am thankful that my pastor was a strong leader. He integrated a spiritual gift assessment into our orientation class when we joined our church. It was not a comprehensive course; it was a one-hour orientation meeting with multiple topics. The rest of my learning about God's divine design, spiritual gifts, and purpose was revealed to me as I grew in my relationship with God, with years of prayer, application, study, teaching, coaching, and training others.

I learned that understanding comes with application. As we apply what we learn and build a relationship with God, we begin to understand—not the other way around. God leads us when we seek Him. Christianity is not a religion; it is a relationship with God our Creator, Jesus our Savior, and the Holy Spirit, our Guide, Advocate, and Helper. It is the Holy Spirit who guides us through this sanctification process.

> Elect according to the foreknowledge of God the Father, through sanctification of the Spirit, unto obedience and sprinkling of the blood of Jesus Christ: Grace unto you, and peace, be multiplied. (1 Peter 1: 2 NKJV)

Every day as we pray, spend time with God, read His Word, and seek to do His will, the Holy Spirit works through us to sanctify us. Sanctify means "to make holy." The Holy Spirit helps us live for God. Sanctification is a lifelong process by which we submit our hearts, minds, and bodies to following Jesus. God loves us so much that He chose us to be His children and become part of His family before we were even born. After we were born, despite our mistakes, sins, or rejection of Him, God covered us with the blood of His Son, Jesus, and redeemed us. God wants us to live with Him for eternity and enjoy His presence.

The Holy Spirit not only sets us free from sin and sanctifies us by working in and through us but also lives in us to help us follow Jesus, serve God, and live in alignment with God's Word and will. As a believer, it is up to you to choose to seek God daily and to prioritize growing in your relationship with God. As a leader, it is up to you to create an atmosphere and culture that fosters individual growth as well as team unity and growth. As a church, it is up to the leaders to help individuals, leaders, and teams grow and become all God designed them to be. Regardless of what barriers you face, take responsibility to align to God's divine design and ignite your potential to be all God designed you to be.

For now, let's talk a little more about what successful leaders do. Why is this important? When leaders are successful and grow, everyone they influence succeeds and grows.

Successful leaders recognize that people are their greatest asset. They see people as opportunities to develop, not as problems. To be a great leader, one needs to love people and develop a heart to serve people. Successful leaders allocate resources, time, and money to develop people. Unsuccessful leaders see people as problems. They dread talking with people or go out of their way to avoid their people. Then they wonder why their people don't do what they say or don't follow them. Unsuccessful leaders don't invest as much in developing their people. I have been fortunate to work with many successful leaders, study leadership, and practice it for nearly thirty years, so I know what successful leaders do and how to help people succeed.

> For God so loved the world that he gave his one
> and only Son, that whoever believes in him shall
> not perish but have eternal life. (John 3:16 NIV)

The Bible tells us that God loves us, and the greatest of all commandments is to love God, receive God's love, and love others. One way to find out how much leaders value their people is to look at their training strategy, plan, budget, and resources. Oftentimes, leaders see training as an expense, or worse, as a tactical program instead of part of the plan to be a good steward of their greatest asset, their people. Successful leaders see training as part of the growth strategy.

High-growth churches and organizations that value their people invest in growing organically. While some churches and organizations grow through acquisition, expanding the number of multi-sites, or planting churches, if they fail to invest in training and teaching their people to apply God's Word, they will not become strong. In a church, the body of the church needs to be equipped and empowered to do the work of God. In an organization, the people need to be equipped and empowered to gain a competitive advantage. One common reason churches fail is due to a lack of leadership. Successful churches equip and empower their people with a spiritual growth pathway; unsuccessful churches do not. Keep in mind, one way to retain members is to provide training and help people grow. Training is essential to retention. God designed His church to grow and multiply!

One reason I am such an advocate of training for growth is because I have learned so much from churches that have a training strategy, plan, and curriculum in classes and small groups to help people grow spiritually. When we grow, we have more to contribute to help others grow. You can't give what you don't have. In addition, as a sales leader, I built winning teams and led more than 120 people. To recruit and retain top talent, training was always a priority. Then I got an MBA and a master's degree in human development, with an emphasis on training and leadership. I joined an organization to build and oversee all the sales and customer education worldwide to scale our company. Designing training to grow enabled us to double our revenue in just two and a half years, instead of our target of five years. In other words, it was training that enabled us to recruit and retain top talent and double our revenue in half the time. I recognize that God's church is a family, not a business. However, the principle of valuing people and investing in growing your church, your leadership team, and yourself is a stewardship principle from the Bible.

What Does the Bible Say?

The Bible tells us that leaders are brokers of gifts and potential.

Prior to becoming a people leader, I worked for great leaders and one not so great leader. I remember saying to myself, "I want to be a great leader." Coupled with learning, my primary spiritual gift is leadership. I began studying leadership to learn what great leaders do.

Successful leaders love people. Since starting my own firm, I have trained and coached hundreds of leaders to become more successful. The unsuccessful leaders don't love their people and don't know their people's needs. If a leader doesn't know their people's needs, how can they add value to their lives and serve them? In addition, many leaders lack a foundation of godly principles to inspire, equip, and empower their employees. As a result, I will be outlining some of these principles to lead yourself, your team, and your organization.

As a leader, you are a broker of gifts and potential. What does that mean? It means that, as a leader, you need to not only use your spiritual gifts, talents, and abilities to honor God but also to help those you work with do the same. You can broker their potential by helping them be all God designed them to be. What does that look like? You would know God's design for your life, be living your purpose, using spiritual gifts and abilities, and experiencing the joy of doing the work of God to bless others. We would be ignited and united, and Christ would be magnified from the altar of our lives. Imagine everyone on your team and in your small group living to their full potential for the glory of God. Everyone is a leader and can ignite their potential and broker the potential of those around them by applying what they learn as they read this book. It is by seeking to know God, learning, applying His Word, and depending on and serving God that He ignites our potential, gives us our purpose, and helps us understand our design as part of His design and the master plan that He created before we were even born.

God wants you to live to the fullest, to ignite your God-given potential, to be a light unto the world, and to push back darkness with the light of the Gospel. Ignite the light of Christ in you! Unite and ignite the light of Christ in His church!

Ifyou are a people leader, with people directly reporting to you, you also need to be a broker of their gifts and potential. *A leader's job is to love people, to develop people, and to build a culture whereby they can ignite people's potential and be all God designed them to be.* Successful leaders see a person's God-given potential and help them see themselves as God sees them. I remember one year, God gave me the words "If you could see what I see!" I believe He wanted me to see the potential in myself and others. As believers, we need to gain a godly perspective to become all He designed us to be.

> *"If you could see what I see!"*

As we seek to know God better, to study His Word, to seek His will, and to love God more, we start to see things from God's perspective instead of our own. God's Word renews our mind. His presence and a relationship with God transform our heart's desires to be more pleasing to Him. When God looks at you, He sees your potential! He sees you as His masterpiece. As we gain God's perspective, it changes how we see people.

Now when I look at people, I see their potential. When I don't see their potential, I ask God to help me see what He sees because I know God sees what you and I can become according to His plan and purpose for our lives. God sees your potential and wants you to be all He designed you to be. To ignite your potential, get in alignment with how God sees you.

A leader's job is to love people, to develop people, and to build a culture whereby they can ignite people's potential to be all God designed them to be. How? By aligning to God's divine design. The Bible is our source and authority. Friends, I promise you that nobody will ever love you, know your every need, and care for you more than God does. He knows your every need, and His road map for life is the Bible. If you haven't already surrendered to His authority, I want to encourage you to pray this prayer:

Prayer:

"Lord, I may not understand all of this, but I give You and Your Word authority over my life. I put my hope and trust in You alone. Teach me what You want to teach me as I read and apply this book. Fill me with wisdom and align my heart to Your heart, Lord. In Jesus's name, I pray. Amen."

I hope by now you realize that this is not a self-help book; instead, it is about becoming all God designed you to be and glorifying God in the process. Everything we have comes from above—our potential, our gifts, our talents, and our purpose. All of these are designed to be used to bless others and glorify God.

We are all leaders. Some of us are in formal leadership roles; others are in informal leadership roles. What is leadership? I learned that leadership is influence, and on average, we influence 60,000 people in our lifetimes. The reality is that we will either influence people in a positive way or negative way. Personally, I want to influence people in a positive way. We lead and influence people all around us, including ourselves, every day through the choices we make.

If you are a parent, you are a leader. If you are a spouse, you are a leader. If you are a sister or a brother, you are a leader. If you are a people leader, you are a leader at work, in the community, and at home. You are influencing people around you every day, everywhere you go. The problem is not everyone is an effective leader who thinks about and works at influencing people in a positive, loving way, in alignment with God's divine design. As we align to God's divine design, God's Word, and God's will, we can positively influence others to know, love, and glorify God. I believe the greatest legacy we can leave is the gift of knowing, loving, and glorifying God. People are not going to remember the car you drove, the title you acquired in your career, or how much money you had, but they will remember how you helped them know and love a God that transformed their life for the better. If we are not intentional about aligning to God's divine design, we won't consistently influence people in a positive way. I decided years ago that I want to have a positive influence on others, build others up, serve others, and help others succeed. It is my intent that by applying the principles in this book, you, too, will choose to align to God's divine design to experience the joy of influencing others positively and glorifying God. Doing so honors God and puts a smile on God's face. God wants us to experience the great wonder of being in His presence and being used by Him daily.

What else does the Bible say? In Matthew 10:1–15, Jesus empowered His disciples by personally calling them by their names, instructing them, giving them a vision for more workers (in Matthew 9:37–38), and sending them out to bless others. Leaders must develop others to reach their potential.

Jesus shares His vision:

Then he said to his disciples, "The harvest is plentiful, but the workers are few. Ask the Lord of the harvest, therefore, to send out workers into his harvest field." (Matthew 9:37–38 NIV)

Why is it that 90 percent of the people in the church are bystanders and only 10 percent or less volunteer and do the work of God? Jesus is calling all of us to be leaders and to serve. God did not design the church for pastors and staff to do all the work. God really spoke to me with this verse. My heart ached to think how few people want to do God's work.

There are times in my life when I have been so busy with work and traveling that I didn't make time to serve. That's not the case anymore. As God matured me spiritually, I made it a priority to serve and give back. I share that with you to encourage you to serve now. Don't wait. God needs you to do His work that He designed you for. This includes discovering, developing, and using your spiritual gifts to serve.

He clearly articulates the need and why it is important. The harvest is plentiful, but the workers are few. God needs you and I to do His work today. God needs an equipped and empowered church body, a family of believers, to fulfill His work. I don't know about you, but I want to be one of those workers. Many people live their

> *God needs you and I to do His work today.*

whole lives never discovering God's design for their life. I hope this book saves you valuable time by learning how important this is and makes it easier for you to discover how you are part of God's epic story and how you fit into doing His work. Here is the good news: God has already designed a plan for you.

> For I know the plans I have for you declares the Lord,
> plans to prosper you and not to harm you, plans to
> give you hope and a future. (Jeremiah 29:11 NIV)

As a body of believers, we are designed to be the hands and feet of Jesus and to do the work of God. The world will tell you that you need to design your own life to be happy or to follow your heart, but that won't bring happiness and joy. God knows that we are to align to His will, His Word, and His heart. That is how we are designed, and that is how we will experience the greatest joy. God wants you to experience joy by being in a relationship with Him, growing, serving, and doing the work of the kingdom for which He designed you.

Align to God's Divine Design

Let's talk about alignment and the benefits of alignment.

What does alignment mean? Alignment means "a position of agreement." There is great power in alignment with God! When we talk about alignment, we are talking about posturing our heart to align with God's heart, learning and growing daily in our relationship with God and the application of His Word, His will, and His direction in our lives.

What are the signs and symptoms of lack of alignment? Signs and symptoms of a lack of alignment can include confusion, division, destruction, sickness, defeat, apathy, and lack of passion, purpose, or clarity, leaving people feeling powerless without hope.

Where have you seen or experienced a lack of alignment? For some of you, it may have been in the workplace; for others, it may have been at church or in your family, a marriage, or a friendship.

Where are you experiencing or seeing confusion, division, sickness, defeat, apathy, or lack of passion, purpose, or clarity? For example, if you are experiencing confusion about what direction to take in the next phase of your life, it could be that you don't know God's purpose and plan for your life. It can also be because you don't know your spiritual gifts, abilities, and sweet spot; thus, you have no filter for sorting out options. Gain clarity by seeking to understand God's purpose for your life, spiritual gifts, and how He wants you to use these to bless others and advance His kingdom. As you complete your profile in the back milestone 5, pray, and seek to understand God's Word, you will gain clarity.

Some people gain clarity instantly; for others, it takes time. Be patient, trust God, and seek to know Him more. One person who was defeated experienced breakthrough as she discovered her spiritual gifts and learned God's purpose for her life. It was like she turned on the faucet to God's presence, power, and passion in her life. Her feelings of defeat disappeared. It was beautiful to see God's presence and power in her after she applied the principles in this book.

When we align with God's design, we experience unity, abundance, clarity, health, victory, encouragement, hope, and empowerment. While we live in a world where not everyone has accepted Jesus as their personal Savior and repented to follow Jesus and serve God, we are designed to be a light unto a dark world and magnify Christ from the altar of our lives.

Jesus said that we must be set apart as He is set apart.

> They are not of the world, just as I am not of the world. Sanctify them by Your truth. Your word is truth. As You sent Me into the world, I also have sent them into the world. And for their sakes I sanctify Myself, that they also may be sanctified by the truth. (John 17:16–19 NKJV)

We are called to be holy, just as God is holy. This means that we are to live our lives differently than those in the world around us.

> But as He who called you is holy, you also be holy in all your conduct, because it is written, "Be holy, for I am holy." (1 Peter 1:15–16 NKJV)

We are going to talk about alignment with God's divine design, God's will, God's Word, and God's plan for your life.

It's important to use the Bible and God's Word, not the outside world, as the source of truth. The world is full of facts but not truth. We need to go to the source, our Creator who designed us, and learn what God's perspective is to see things from a biblical point of view.

> And be not conformed to this world: but be transformed by the renewing of your mind, that you may prove what is that good and acceptable and perfect will of God. (Romans 12:2 NKJV)

Alignment also means posturing our heart to God—loving God with our whole heart, mind, and soul. The goal is heart-level change, but God often uses our very actions to form our hearts. He also uses our hearts to form our actions. Our hearts matter most, but our actions matter too. Our actions not only reflect our hearts; they shape our hearts.

Who modeled alignment better than anyone? Jesus. Jesus was in perfect alignment with God's Word and God's will, and He demonstrated that in His daily actions. Jesus was obedient to God's Word and His will. As He faced fear and trepidation, as He anticipated the unbearable suffering He would experience on the cross, He prayed to the Father for the strength to carry out His will.

> Saying, Father, if it is Your will, take this cup away from Me; nevertheless not My will, but Yours, be done. (Luke 22:42 NKJV)

Jesus aligned His heart's posture to the Father's will, even unto death on the cross.

Learning to trust God and align to God's divine design is a lifelong process, and it starts by inviting Jesus to be our Savior and Lord of our lives, repenting of our sins, and being in a relationship with God by studying God's Word and seeking to know God better.

The good news is that we are not alone. The Holy Spirit, our helper, guide, and advocate, is inside of us and empowers us to overcome any obstacle in aligning to God's divine design, Word, and will.

Partnering with God to do God's will and God's work, and inviting the Holy Spirit in to help you, is possible for every believer. Alignment is not a *sometimes* thing but rather a daily process of knowing God better, worshipping God, praying, reading, and understanding His Word and His will for our lives. As we begin to know God, love God, and receive His love, we trust Him more.

The Benefits of Alignment

What are the benefits of alignment with God's will and God's Word?

1. *Alignment with God produces fruit.* This means that we only bear fruit when we remain in God, and God in us. We need to be aligned and connecting with God to bear fruit. What does this mean? It means our outward actions result from our heart being aligned to God's heart. Fruit can include the love of God flowing through us to be kind, compassionate toward the needs of others, gentle, humble, and able to exhibit the fruits of the Spirit, serving as salt and light to a world in need of Jesus. This is not something we do with our own power; instead, the Holy Spirit transforms us to become like Christ.

   "I am the vine; you are the branches. If you remain in me and I in you, you will bear much fruit; apart from me you can do nothing." (John 15:5 NIV)

2. *Alignment provides success and joy while igniting our potential.* When we know and acknowledge God's plans and design, we allow Him to direct our steps toward success, joy, and the fulfillment of our God-given potential to honor God. God is life, so the closer we get to God, the more passionate we become. You will become a bright light, full of life. People will say, "Something is different

about you." They will see the light of Christ in you and say, "Something is special about you."

> The Spirit of God has made me, And the breath of the Almighty gives me life. (Job 33:4 NKJV)

3. *Alignment helps us win.* As Christians, alignment allows us to unite and ignite our God-given potential to live in victory because of Jesus, the Messiah. This means living in alignment with God's Word and will leads us to victory, not defeat. Without alignment to God's will and God's Word, we will never fulfill our God-given potential to be all God designed us to be. Are you living from a place of victory or defeat? God wants us to win, to live from a place of victory per the finished work on the cross. You were designed to win!

> "I have told you these things, so that in me you may have peace. In this world you will have trouble. But take heart! I have overcome the world." (John 16:33 NIV)

4. *Alignment releases the blessings of heaven.* Alignment is an expression of our love for God. It releases God's power, unity, transformation, healing, blessings, peace, and empowerment to believers. Alignment demonstrates our humility and keeps God first place in our lives. Humility is often misunderstood. Humility is not thinking less of ourselves. Instead, it is thinking of ourselves less. God is the source of everything we have.

> Humble yourselves before the Lord, and he will lift you up. (James 4:10 NIV)

5. *Alignment to God's will and God's Word provides wisdom.* From where does our wisdom flow, and where does the credit go? I know all good things that flow from me come

from God and that I am simply a vessel. Alignment to God's will and Word provides us with wisdom for daily living. Everything we need for success and all the wisdom we need for life comes from God's will and God's Word.

> The proverbs of Solomon son of David, king of Israel: for gaining wisdom and instruction; for understanding words of insight; (Proverbs 1:1–2 NIV)

6. *Alignment to God's will and God's Word provides healing.* God wants you well. Let's get into alignment, also called agreement, with His Word and His will so you can receive healing. Jesus was perfectly aligned to God's will and God's Word. Because of Jesus, we are healed.

> Who Himself bore our sins in His own body on the tree, that we, having died to sins, might live for righteousness—by whose stripes you were healed. (1 Peter 2:24 NKJV)

7. *Alignment to God's will and God's Word transforms us.* This is so important because reading and applying God's Word and engaging in prayer time renews our mind with God's perspective. The truth will set you free, if you know it. Align to God's will and Word to be transformed into the image of Christ.

> Create in me a clean heart, O God, And renew a steadfast spirit within me. (Psalm 51:10 NKJV)

8. *Alignment to God's will and God's Word brings unity.* Where there is Jesus, there is unity. When Jesus is absent, there is division. Let's shift our eyes to Jesus and align with God's will and God's Word to create unity in our relationships, family, community, and our church.

> How good and pleasant it is when God's
> people live together in unity! (Psalm 133:1 NIV)

9. *Alignment to God's will and God's Word brings empowerment.* What does empowerment mean? It means to transfer authority. God does not tell us what to do; He loves us so much that He gives us choices. He gives us authority to choose and equips us to do everything He calls us to do. That's true love.

> That Christ may dwell in your hearts through
> faith; that you, being rooted and grounded in
> love. (Ephesians 3:17 NKJV)

10. *Alignment to God's will and God's Word brings restoration.* Restoration is a repeated theme throughout the Bible. For something to be restored, it must have previously died or been broken or harmed in some way. Jesus is the only one who can restore everything back to God's divine design. Jesus will not only restore your life to its previous level, but He will restore it to a level you never imagined possible. Restoration can take place physically, spiritually, financially, emotionally, and relationally.

> After Job had prayed for his friends, the LORD
> restored his fortunes and gave him twice as
> much as he had before. (Job 42:10 NIV)

All these benefits of alignment are available to you! God wants to give you these benefits and more. We must recognize the importance of using the Bible and God's Word, not the outside world, as the source of truth. Why is this important? Because the Bible is our road map for life. It is our instructional guide, full of God's truth. The world will not provide any of these benefits. In fact, Satan's goal is to steal, kill, and destroy. The enemy does not want you to align to God's divine design. He opposes God and is the father of lies, deception, doubt, slander, and destruction. If

Susan A. Lund

you think or feel any of those feelings as you read this book, know this: God overcame Satan's power of death, and as a believer, you can resist the devil, and he will flee from you.

> Submit yourselves, then, to God. Resist the devil,
> and he will flee from you. (James 4:7 NIV)

To get rid of those attacks from the enemy, exercise the authority God has given you to defeat the enemy. You can simply say, "No, Satan. I submit myself to God and resist you. In the name of Jesus, away from me, Satan! Flee!" The Word of God is a sword to combat the strategy, plans, and tactics of the enemy.

> You, dear children, are from God and have overcome them, because the one who is in you is greater than the one who is in the world. (1 John 4:4 NIV)

Potential must begin inside of you before it can manifest outside of you. It's your job to discover, develop, and distribute what God has placed inside of you to add value to and bless others for God's glory.

If you are a leader, as you learn, understand, and experience God's divine design for your life, you can model it for your team and organization. When you are a leader, people will follow what you do more than what you say. It's an inside-out process.

Successful leaders who need a plan to ignite potential in themselves, in those who work with them, and in those who attend their church may use this book as a tool to inspire, equip, and empower individuals, teams, and their church to ignite their potential and be all God designed you to be.

Whether you are a pastor, a church leader, or an individual reading this book, my intent is that you will benefit and grow spiritually and that you will use what you learn to grow God's church and to advance God's kingdom. My prayer is that you will learn how you can ignite your God-given potential, find your purpose, and discover, develop, and align to God's divine design for your life to become all God wants you to be.

This is intended to be an application book with questions that encourage you to write down what you learn and how you can apply it. You will retain more by participating and writing out your answers. You will be able to refer to your notes to share what you learned with others.

Why is that so important? God wants us to be doers of the Word:

> Do not merely listen to the word, and so deceive yourselves. Do what it says. (James 1:22 NIV)

My intent is that you will be a doer of God's Word and will.

Why? Because that is how you will benefit most. Understanding comes with application. Applying what you learn allows you to receive the blessings that come from being a doer of the Word. It's also how you will bless others.

Lastly, when you hear the Word of God, the enemy tries to steal it. When you apply it, it moves from your head to your heart to your body. The enemy can't steal that because it becomes a part of you. That's why it is so important to study, memorize scripture, meditate on it, speak it, and apply it. That feeds the Spirit of God in you and embeds the Word of God—the truth—into your soul, mind, heart, and emotions, so that it can rise up, grow, and move into your body. It helps you apply God's Word and live it out.

Remember, understanding comes through application. Answer these questions as an individual. Then, if you are in a small group, discuss them as a group.

Prayer:

"Holy Spirit, reveal to me what You want me to know, say, or do as a result of what I have learned. Give me eyes to see, ears to hear, and an open heart to receive whatever You want to show me. I want to know You and love You more, Lord. In Jesus's name, I pray. Amen."

Discovery and Application Questions: Align to God's Divine Design and Ignite Your Potential!

1. What did I learn?

2. What does the Holy Spirit want me to do today?

3. What can I apply or do to align to God's divine design?

Don't extinguish your potential! Instead, take action to ignite your God-given potential, serve others, and be all God designed you to be. As a leader in your church, you may use this book as a resource to ignite the potential in your church to become all God designed you to be.

Let's talk about your spiritual gifts and answer the following five questions.

1. What is a spiritual gift?
2. Why is it important to understand and discover your spiritual gifts?
3. What happens if I don't discover and use my spiritual gifts?
4. What are the benefits of discovering and using my spiritual gifts?
5. How can I discover my spiritual gifts?

Where does the word gift *come from?* The word *gift* in the New Testament is the Greek word "Charismata," which means "gifts of grace," and refers to the gifts or special abilities God has given believers through the Holy Spirit. They originate not from us but from the Holy Spirit.

What is the definition of a spiritual gift? Lets' first talk about what they are not. Spiritual gifts are not the same as the gift of the Holy Spirit. There are many gifts of the Spirit, but there is only one Holy Spirit. The gift of the Holy Spirit is received the moment a person trusts Christ as their Savior. Simon Peter said this to the multitudes on the day of Pentecost:

> Peter replied, "Repent and be baptized, every one of you, in the name of Jesus Christ for the forgiveness of your sins. And you will receive the gift of the Holy Spirit. The promise is for you and your children and for all who are far off—for all whom the Lord our God will call." (Acts 2:38-39 NIV)

What is a spiritual gift, and what does the Bible teach us about spiritual gifts? Spiritual gifts are the natural or supernatural abilities God gives every believer to serve the body of Christ, the church. Spiritual gifts are expressed through the direction of the Holy Spirit in the lives of Christian believers.

I believe they are to be used for God's work, to advance God's kingdom and to bring the light of Christ to a dark world, according to His vision and mission, to reach all people with the Gospel of Christ. I believe they are used to build up and strengthen God's church and advance His kingdom.

I encourage you to read this definition out loud three times so that it sinks in. Remember, understanding comes with application. If you are not going to do it for yourself, do it for others. When you talk to others about spiritual gifts, they will ask you what a spiritual gift is. You want to be ready with an answer.

What about nonbelievers? Do they receive spiritual gifts? No. Nonbelievers do not receive spiritual gifts. I learned this the hard way. I'll never forget when someone pulled me aside and asked me, "So what is a spiritual gift anyway?" I explained what a spiritual gift was, and when I was done, they looked me square in the eye and said, "I have no idea what you're talking about. I don't even know the words you're using or what they mean." This stopped me in my tracks. I was so humbled. I didn't know this person was an unbeliever. I don't initiate conversations like this in the workplace. After hearing that response, in my humility, I got on my knees and prayed for six months: "God, help me to be more effective in communicating what a spiritual gift is and in how I communicate to nonbelievers." I know God is in charge and the Holy Spirit works through us in these conversations, and I am simply a vessel. At the same time, I want to take responsibility to be prepared to help people succeed. I want to be ready and equipped to be used by God. I also want to help people realize and ignite their God-given potential because that is how they will experience the greatest joy.

God made it very clear what I needed to do. He directs our steps. You see, most people tell me that I am very articulate and speak clearly. When someone said they had no idea what I was saying, that revealed to me that this conversation was directed by God for His purposes. God really does direct our steps when we ask Him to.

Shortly thereafter, God answered my prayer, which He always does. My pastor gave a sermon and asked us to pray for the Holy Spirit to reveal to us what He wanted us to do. So that afternoon, I prayed, "Holy Spirit, what is it that You want me to do?" Immediately, I got an answer. The Holy Spirit gave me two very specific instructions: 1) go talk with the pastor and 2) give a Bible to a nonbeliever.

Both were uncomfortable, but I did them anyway. I remember talking with our pastor. You see, I was new to the church and didn't know him, other than seeing him and listening to his teaching on Sunday. He asked me, "What brings you here?"

I replied, "You said, 'Go home and ask the Holy Spirit in prayer, "What do you want me to do?"' so I did. The Holy Spirit sent me to you." After a great conversation, he sent me to another pastor. At the end of that conversation, the pastor asked me to create and teach a course on spiritual gifts for the entire church. I was so excited I nearly jumped out of my chair because I knew this was an answer to prayer. I then spent another seven months researching spiritual gifts and how to explain them to believers and nonbelievers. After teaching a spiritual gifts course at our church multiple times, I did another two years of research to write this book. Here is what I learned:

1. *We are always in progress, including myself.* Life is a journey with God whereby God continues to teach us and transform us.

2. *God's Word doesn't always make sense if you don't have God in you.* We need to first choose to believe, repent, and receive by inviting Jesus into our hearts as our Savior to be the Lord of our life. Why? Because the enemy blindfolds unbelievers to not understand and see the truth. When

they accept Jesus as their Savior, repent of their sins, and commit to live for the Lord, they are set free to see the truth.

> But the natural man does not receive the things of the Spirit of God, for they are foolishness to him; nor can he know them, because they are spiritually discerned. (1 Corinthians 2:14 NKJV)

Nonbelievers don't have spiritual gifts because these gifts are for God's purposes. It is the gift inside the gift. We will look at this in more depth.

The main purpose of spiritual gifts is to edify (build up), exhort (encourage), and comfort the church. We will look at the seven purposes of spiritual gifts in the next chapter. The Bible says, the truth will set you free. Truth will only set you free if you know the truth.

> And you shall know the truth, and the truth shall make you free. (John 8:32 NKJV)

> Pilate therefore said to Him, "Are You a king then?" Jesus answered, "You say rightly that I am a king. For this cause I was born, and for this cause I have come into the world, that I should bear witness to the truth. Everyone who is of the truth hears My voice." (John 18:37 NKJV)

3. *So can a nonbeliever receive spiritual gifts?* No. A nonbeliever can only receive spiritual gifts only by becoming a believer.

How does that work? What separates man from God is sin. As a result, we are no longer with God; we are separated. When we are separated from God, it's like we all have a hole in our hearts before we are believers. We may try to fill that hole in our hearts with other things like money, work, exercise, or, in some cases, drugs, alcohol, and other destructive things.

However, the only way to fill that hole is by accepting Jesus Christ as our Savior. You see, when we were separated from God by sin, He sent His only Son, Jesus, to die on the cross, to stand in the gap of our sin so we could be with God for eternity.

The Bible tells us Jesus is the way, the truth, and the life:

Jesus answered, "I am the way and the truth and the life. No one comes to the Father except through me." (John 14:6 NIV)

When we accept Jesus as our Savior, He fills that hole. Jesus creates that bridge for a nonbeliever to gain access to salvation and be with God forever.

What does the word *salvation* mean? Salvation is deliverance from danger or suffering. To save is to deliver or protect. The word carries the idea of victory, health, or preservation. As Christians, we are saved from "wrath"— that is, from God's judgment of sin (Romans 5:9; 1 Thessalonians 5:9). Why? Because sin separated us from God and created death. God removed the consequences of sin and death by sending His only Son, Jesus, to die on the cross so that we can have eternal life and be forgiven of our sins when we become believers.

It was Jesus's death on the cross and resurrection that achieved our salvation, as outlined in Romans 5:10 and Ephesians 1:7. We didn't do anything to earn this; instead, God gave it to us as a gift that is available through faith in

Jesus Christ. Salvation is available to anyone. No matter what you have done, God loves you and wants to have a relationship with you.

What happens when we accept the gift of salvation from God? Are we born again? God gives us eternal life and a home in heaven so we can be with God forever. God also makes us new inside. He gives us a new heart, a new beginning, and a better life. He places the Holy Spirit inside of us to guide us and be our advocate. God gives us a spiritual gift that operates under the direction of the Holy Spirit to do what He designed us to do.

In summary, a nonbeliever can receive spiritual gifts after they choose to believe, trust, and accept Jesus as their Savior, repent of their sins, and depend on God for provision, assurance, and security. If you have not already done that, you can do so through the salvation prayer here. You don't have to understand everything; simply pray the salvation prayer.

If you are not yet a Christian and you want protection from the dangers of sin and want to receive the blessings God has for you, you can say a simple prayer. If you are a Christian and want to renew your commitment to God, you, too, can say this prayer.

Salvation Prayer:

"Father, it is written in Your Word that if I confess with my mouth that Jesus is Lord and believe in my heart that You have raised Him from the dead, I shall be saved.

Therefore, Father, I confess that Jesus is my Lord. I invite Him to be the Lord of my life right now. Please come into my heart as my Lord and Savior. I know I am a sinner, repent of my sins, and ask for

Your forgiveness. Thank You for forgiving me. I put my hope and trust in You and give You complete control of my life. Old things have passed away; now all things become new in Jesus's name, I pray. Amen."

Through that simple prayer, an unbeliever can be saved and spend eternity with God.

Why is it so important to discover, develop, and align to God's divine design?

Did you know that individuals and congregations become spiritually impotent when the members do not freely and responsibly allow the Holy Spirit to manifest God's ministry and power through the gifts He has given?

We are designed to live spiritually potent, productive, and purposeful lives that honor God and advance His kingdom. Now is the time to ignite your potential, to be all God designed you to be.

The Bible tells us that there will be a great spiritual awakening before Jesus returns. Every awakening, including the Tribulation awakening, as described in Revelation 14:4, begins with a dedicated few. The Bible describes the group that will ignite this awakening:

> These are the ones who were not defiled with women, for they are virgins. These are the ones who follow the Lamb wherever He goes. These were redeemed from among men, being firstfruits to God and to the Lamb. (Revelation 14:4 NKJV)

You see, there are two gifts. The first gift is the gift of salvation. It is at that time of conversion that the Holy Spirit takes up residence in us, and He will take up residence in you once you have prayed that prayer and accepted Jesus as your Savior. Then God gives us our second gift, our spiritual gift or gifts for His purposes. As a child of God, we become part of His family.

When I think of a spiritual gift, I think of it as the gift inside the gift. The greatest gift God gives us is salvation and eternal life. We received the gift of being with God forever. What a great God we have!

> For the wages of sin is death, but the gift of God is eternal life in Christ Jesus our Lord. (Romans 6:23 NKJV)

We need to accept and receive that gift first. With salvation, God forgives all our sins. It doesn't matter what you have done; God forgives you and gives you a new beginning.

When we accept the gift of salvation, God starts a process in us called sanctification. God places the Holy Spirit inside of us when we accept Jesus Christ as our personal Lord and Savior.

> Jesus answered, "Most assuredly, I say to you, unless one is born of water and the Spirit, he cannot enter the kingdom of God." (John 3:5 NKJV)

> But you are not in the flesh but in the Spirit, if indeed the Spirit of God dwells in you. Now if anyone does not have the Spirit of Christ, he is not His. (Romans 8:9 NKJV)

As the Holy Spirit comes to live inside us after we accept the first gift of salvation, God gives us at least one spiritual gift.

Thus, *spiritual gift* has no meaning to an unbeliever because they don't receive it until they accept the first gift.

Jesus shared with His disciples that He was going away and that He would send a Helper. God then placed another gift inside of us—the Holy Spirit. The Holy Spirit is our Helper, Guide, Advocate, and Counselor.

> "But very truly I tell you, it is for your good that I am going away. Unless I go away, the Advocate will not come to you; but if I go, I will send him to you." (John 16:7 NIV)

> "Very truly I tell you, whoever believes in me will do the works I have been doing, and they will do even greater things than these, because I am going to the Father." (John 14:12 NIV)

> Now to each one the manifestation of the Spirit is given for the common good. (Corinthians 12:7 NIV)

Each of you has been blessed with one of God's many wonderful gifts to be used in the service of others. Be sure to use your gift well.

> Once you were not a people, but now you are the people of God; once you had not received mercy, but now you have received mercy. (1 Peter 2:10 NIV)

This means that you, born again, have the Holy Spirit inside you. The Holy Spirit is with you 24-7 to help you, to guide you, to be your advocate in your daily walk with God as you use your gifts to bless others and serve God.

Why Are Spiritual Gifts Important?

To steward what God has given us to bless others and glorify God.

One thing I have learned since I became a Christian is that there is a lot of information and teaching on salvation but not as much on stewardship. There is a big difference between the two. At the end of our lives, we will be asked two questions and need to give an account to God:

1. What did you do with Jesus?
2. What did you do with what I gave you?

Let's unpack each of these.

We are ultimately accountable to God for the answer to both questions. How you answer the first question—"What did you do with Jesus?"—determines whether you are saved, which determines your eternal destination. Will you go to heaven to be with God for eternity? If you accept Jesus Christ as your personal Savior, you will be with God for eternity.

If you have not accepted Jesus as your personal Savior, you still can. It is not too late. If you have a family member or friend who is lost, it's not too late for them to accept Jesus, to be forgiven of their sins and saved. No matter what you have done or what mistakes you have made, God loves you and wants you to be with Him forever. The choice to be with God for eternity is yours.

The second question is "What did you do with what I gave you?" Romans 14:12 tells us that we will each give an account to God. Your answer will determine your eternal reward. This is all about trusting God, obeying God, being a good steward of what He has given you, and fulfilling His purpose and plan for your life. Discovering and developing your spiritual gifts and aligning to His divine design to serve God is all part of stewarding what God has given you. I have a personal motto: I don't ever want to say, "I wish I could have, should have, would have." In other words, I don't want to look back and say, "I wish I would have trusted God more." Instead, I want to say, "I gave it my all. I took bold steps of faith and did what God asked me or said to do." Writing this book was one of those bold steps of faith, depending on God every step of the way.

I remember our pastor teaching on stewardship about twenty years ago. From listening to him and taking notes, I learned that we never really own anything; we are simply borrowing it or using what God gives us while we are here on earth. We won't take anything with us to heaven except God's Word and our character. He went on to say that we will lose everything we have: our home, our belongings, our cars, our money. None of that will matter. What matters most is aligning our hearts to God and our life to God's divine design to steward what He gives us for His glory.

I learned five spiritual practices to help steward what He gives us.

1. Make it a priority to know God better and love God more every day.
2. Steward what God gives you well to bless others and honor God.
3. Hold on to things loosely, recognizing that they are not yours, and be ready to step into whatever God wants you to do next. Everything belongs to God. Let God lead you out of your comfort zone to become who He wants you to become.
4. Understand God's purpose, design, and plan for your life and work toward fulfilling it every day out of love for God. Find your sweet spot to have maximum impact for God. Multiply and grow what God gives you, including your spiritual gifts, talents, abilities, and everything He provides, by being in a relationship with God, knowing God, and loving God more daily.
5. Seek to establish an eternal perspective and invest in what will be around for eternity, which is God's people and God's church. Serve others and advance God's church, which is His family, because that honors God.

If sanctification is not a common word for you, let's walk through what it means. Sanctification does not happen with one prayer like salvation; rather, sanctification is a lifelong journey.

During this journey, God transforms our character to make us like Him. God sets us free from habitual sin, purifies our hearts, and empowers us to fulfill the purpose for which He created us. I see it as a great adventure!

We all move through this process at different paces depending on how much we surrender to God, seek to know God, understand His Word, and align to God's divine design for us.

Discovering your unique design helps you embrace what God is doing and wants to do in and through you. When I say *design*, I am talking about how God designed you and what God wants you to become—all that God designed you to be. I am talking about living a blessed live that is aligned with the will of God and the Word of God. All of this happens by being in a relationship with God, knowing God, loving God, trusting God, and obeying God as we walk with Him daily.

Spiritual gifts are a grace and anointing that are given to each person through the Holy Spirit. They are designed like an ability to be a point of leverage for each believer. The purpose of spiritual gifts is to edify (build up), exhort (encourage), and comfort the church.

When you use your spiritual gifts for this purpose, the kingdom of God advances. You experience great joy and God's presence and power, and you honor God. To do so, we need to spend time with God to know God, God's Word, and God's will so we can be a vessel for Him to serve others and grow God's church. Why? Because that is how God designed us, to live according to His design, which magnifies Christ from the altar of our life.

> But the manifestation of the Spirit is given to each
> one for the profit of all. (1 Corinthians 12:7 NKJV)

God has given each of you a gift from His great variety of spiritual gifts. Use them well to serve one another and honor God.

> Each of you should use whatever gift you have
> received to serve others, as faithful stewards of
> God's grace in its various forms. (1 Peter 4:10 NIV)

I believe stewardship is an aspect of leadership. Successful leaders don't focus on themselves. Instead, God calls us to lead by focusing on the needs of others, to use what we are given to serve others and help them satisfy their needs out of love for the glory of God. God gives us these gifts because He knows we need them to fulfill the mission of the church and to do the work of God today and in the days to come.

What happens if you don't discover and use your spiritual gifts? Let's walk through five consequences of failing to use our gifts.

Five Consequences of Failing to Use Our Gifts

What does the Bible say?

A few years ago, I read through the entire Bible a couple of times. I have read and studied the Bible all my adult life, but I didn't understand it as well as I wanted to. Joining a small group and reading and discussing it really increased my understanding. I learned that I needed to consume more of God's Word and apply it so I could understand it better. I needed to see the big picture, *His story*, and how it all fit together to understand it. The more I read, the more I wanted to read. I also learned that the Bible is full of daily instruction on what to do and what not to do. It outlines the consequences, which I really appreciate.

I love the word *consequences*. Why? Because consequences help us make good choices and protect us. They create a healthy boundary of protection, just like lanes on the road. Lanes prevent us from going off the road. If we go outside of the lane on the right side, we can drive into a ditch or a guardrail. If we go outside the left of the lane without signaling, we can get into an accident.

The word *consequence* means the effect or outcome of something that occurred earlier. Consequences protect us. I do a lot of work with leaders, training them to be great. One thing that separates great leaders from unsuccessful leaders is that great leaders communicate clear expectations and clear consequences. Unsuccessful leaders are afraid to state clear expectations and consequences, then get frustrated when their people don't do what they want them to do. As I built multiple high-performance teams, studied, and practiced leadership for years, I wanted to do the best for my people. Out of love and concern for their best interests, I communicated consequences with expectations. I learned that people really appreciate clear expectations and consequences. I believe people want to do good work, and they can become more if they work with great leaders.

Who is our model for successful leadership? God and Jesus. God is a superior leader! So is Jesus. God does a great job communicating what happens if we fail to use our gifts properly. I hope as we walk through this, you will receive God's loving intent to protect us and know that these consequences are designed to help us make good choices that glorify God, bless you, and protect you.

> If anyone speaks, they should do so as one who
> speaks the very words of God. If anyone serves,
> they should do so with the strength God provides,
> so that in all things God may be praised through
> Jesus Christ. To him be the glory and the power for
> ever and ever. Amen. (1 Peter 4:11 NIV)

There is a need to lead. We are called to use our gifts to serve others as faithful stewards of God's grace. Those are supernatural abilities God gives each Christ follower, but the general idea of blessing others also carries over to talents. Our talents are also part of God's divine design.

God doesn't give us anything just for our own benefit. Everything we have is for God, to be used to do the work of God and serve others. It all starts with God and is to be used in alignment with God's Word and God's will.

Let's review five consequences for not using our spiritual gifts.

1. *We are disobedient. It's that simple.* The number one takeaway I had as I read the Bible was to obey God. The word *obey* jumped off the page. Disobedience will not protect us; it will put us at risk. God is teaching me that to please God, we need to obey Him, even if it doesn't make sense. How do we do that? Through faith. It was through faith that Noah built an ark to save his family from the flood. He obeyed God.

    > By faith Noah, when warned about things not yet
    > seen, in holy fear built an ark to save his family. By
    > his faith he condemned the world and became heir
    > of the righteousness that is in keeping with faith.
    > (Hebrews 11:7 NIV)

    I don't ever want to intentionally disobey God. The reality is that to do that, I need to know God better and love God more. To consistently obey God, I need to continually learn, study, and apply what God reveals to me in His Word, in prayer, and through the Holy Spirit. The Bible is very clear about discovering, developing, and using our spiritual gifts to do the work of God. So it is out of love for God that we want to be obedient.

2. *The body of Christ suffers.* If we don't used our gifts to build the church body and to glorify God, the body of Christ suffers, which leads us to the third consequence. Not growing up in a church, I didn't know how important it was to build up, strengthen, and grow God's church. Because spiritual gifts operate under the direction of the Holy Spirit, not using our spiritual gifts creates impotence. Congregations that don't

teach on spiritual gifts and how to develop them and put them to use in alignment with God's divine design become spiritually impotent. That is the opposite of what God wants. God calls us to be strong, to lead, and to do the work of God. The Bible says, "let us not be uninformed."

> Now about the gifts of the Spirit, brothers and sisters, I do not want you to be uninformed. (1 Corinthians 12:1 NIV)

Because I am more mature in my relationship with God and understanding of His Word today than I was twenty years ago, serving God's church and advancing the kingdom of God has become a top priority in my life. At the same time, growing in both areas is a lifelong process. The more I learn, the more I realize I have more to learn. For me, it is more about the application of what is learned and the posturing of my heart to desire to know God better and love God more every day than the knowledge alone.

3. *God is not glorified. And when God is not glorified, the church is not multiplied.* God placed a sense of urgency in me to strengthen and grow His family. Of all the times, the time is now. We live in a world that needs the light of Christ. In the Bible, God calls us to leadership to do the work of Christ. You can make a difference by using your spiritual gifts to strengthen God's family of believers in the church, in your community, in your family, and in everyone you interact with.

Some people reject their spiritual gifts and don't think they can be of value to God or deny that they have gifts. When you deny that you have spiritual gifts or reject your gifts, you deny God in you. When you think you can't be of value to God, you are believing a lie. That's exactly what the enemy, Satan, wants you to believe. Every person is valued by God, and every believer has a spiritual gift and can serve God and strengthen

His church. You are so valuable to God that He sent His only Son to die so you can have eternal life.

> For God so loved the world that He gave His only begotten Son, that whoever believes in Him should not perish but have everlasting life. (John 3:16 NKJV)

4. *God's church is not multiplied.* According to Lifeway Research, about 2.56 billion people worldwide will identify with as a Christian by mid-2022. Think about all the churches across the world, in our country, or in your state that have declining membership, participation, and engagement. God's church is an organism, not a business. Our physical body has life. Life makes our body an organism. The church is the body of Christ that depends on life. Christ is our life, and Christ lives in the members of His body. Where there is Christ, there is life. God designed us to grow and multiply by His people, the church body. Let's unite and ignite the light of Christ around the world to advance God's kingdom.

   Romans 9:21, 23 tells us that we are vessels, containers. God is the fountain of life, as stated in John 1:4, which says that in Him, the one who is in the Word and God Himself, there is life. Life is in Him, so He is the tree of life.

   I can't help but ask, "Is your church igniting the God-given potential to be a vessel for the work of God? Are you teaching people to discover, develop, and use their spiritual gifts and making it easy for people to strengthen the church body so it can be empowered to multiply and grow? Can everyone in your small group, your circle of influence, and your family describe what the Bible says about spiritual gifts, why they are important, and their plan for using them to do the work of God and serve others?" If the answer is no, you have some work to do. I respectfully challenge you to apply the principles in this book and what God reveals to you to serve others, glorify God, and ignite your potential. You are valuable; God's church needs what you have to contribute! Join a small group or team to serve and make a difference in the lives of others!

Is there a spiritual development path and education on God's divine design? Does everyone know how special they are and how, as believers, they have been given supernatural abilities to advance His kingdom? I believe this is essential for God's church to be inspired and equipped to do the work of God and be all God designed us to be! Multiplication will follow when we strengthen the body of believers to be vessels for God.

In Matthew 9:35–38, Jesus calls people to leadership, stating the workers are few.

> Jesus went through all the towns and villages, teaching in their synagogues, proclaiming the good news of the kingdom and healing every disease and sickness. When he saw the crowds, he had compassion on them, because they were harassed and helpless, like sheep without a shepherd. Then he said to his disciples, "The harvest is plentiful but the workers are few. Ask the Lord of the harvest, therefore, to send out workers into his harvest field." (Matthew 9:35–38 NIV)

Imagine what would happen if you shared what you learn with others.

Imagine if everyone in your small group, family, and church discovered, developed, and aligned to God's divine design. God's church would be strengthened and multiplied.

God designed His church, His family, to use their spiritual gifts under the direction of the Holy Spirit to build up His church and serve others.

What would happen to our church body if everyone knew their spiritual gifts and used God's supernatural power to strengthen our church body, build His kingdom, and serve?

Think about the impact we could have! God wants us to multiply what He has given us.

Peter goes on to talk about what it means to live for God.

> Therefore, since Christ suffered in his body, arm yourselves also with the same attitude, because whoever suffers in the body is done with sin. As a result, they do not live the rest of their earthly lives for evil human desires, but rather for the will of God. For you have spent enough time in the past doing what pagans choose to do—living in debauchery, lust, drunkenness, orgies, carousing and detestable idolatry. They are surprised that you do not join them in their reckless, wild living, and they heap abuse on you. But they will have to give account to him who is ready to judge the living and the dead. For this is the reason the gospel was preached even to those who are now dead, so that they might be judged according to human standards in regard to the body, but live according to God in regard to the spirit.
>
> The end of all things is near. Therefore be alert and of sober mind so that you may pray. Above all, love each other deeply, because love covers over a multitude of sins. Offer hospitality to one another without grumbling. Each of you should use whatever gift you have received to serve others, as faithful stewards of God's grace in its various forms. If anyone speaks, they should do so as one who speaks the very words of God. If anyone serves,

they should do so with the strength God provides, so that in all things God may be praised through Jesus Christ. To him be the glory and the power for ever and ever. Amen. (1 Peter 4–11 NIV)

God grows His church by people living for God and doing the work of God.

5. *We experience a deficit of joy.* What's the difference between happiness and joy? Happiness is here today and gone tomorrow. It doesn't last! Joy is eternal. It lasts forever! Joy comes with a relationship with God. Don't settle for a fleeting moment of happiness when you can experience joy! God loves you so much He wants you to experience the joy of knowing God, using your gifts to serve others and advance the kingdom of God.

When I am prioritizing where I invest my time, these questions have helped me stay focused on doing the work of God in my daily life.

- Is this an investment into eternity? Will it be here for eternity? In other words, is training leaders to be successful and developing people so they can have a positive influence on others something that will last forever? Yes. God wants us to invest in serving others. Helping others honors God.
- Is what I invest my resources, time, talent, abilities, and gifts in going to be pleasing to God and advance His kingdom?
  - If it does not honor God, I don't want to invest my time in it. One of the things I love to do is read. This question helps me choose books that I can learn from and apply, that enrich my life so I can add value to the lives of others. That honors God.
  - It also helps me say no to TV and social media, which don't enrich my life or honor God.

Next, let's review the benefits.

Five Benefits of Discovering and Using Your Spiritual Gifts

1. *It will help me honor God.* Discovering and using your gifts makes God smile. God blesses us with joy when we honor God with our gifts and life. There is nothing more gratifying than honoring and showing God glory. God made us to feel and experience the greatest gratification when we are in relationship with Him and honor Him.

2. *It will help me be a good steward of the gifts God gave me.* While I shared some of this previously, I believe it is worth repeating because it is so important. There are two approaches to life. The first approach is ownership—thinking we own everything and what we have belongs to us and is for us. The second approach is stewardship. We don't own anything; instead, everything we have is from God and to be used for God. In other words, we are here on this earth for a short time; we are to steward what we have as a gift from God to be used for God and to bless others.

   Don't hold tightly to things of this world, but instead strive to honor God and bless others with what we have been blessed with. Let what God gives you flow through you to bless others. That helps us be open to where God is leading us next.

3. *It will help me to do the work of God and glorify God.*

   Many are the plans in a person's heart,
   but it is the LORD's purpose that prevails.
   (Proverbs 19:21 NIV)

   You may be in a season where you are experiencing challenges because your plan has not worked out. Sometimes God closes one door to open another. I have learned to focus on God's plan and purpose instead of my own. Why? Because the Lord's purpose and plan will prevail. God's ways are always higher than our ways. Personally, I find it comforting to know that God knows my every need more than I do. Trusting God's plan is better than trusting my own plan. Remember, God created a purpose and plan for our lives before we were even born. Who do you trust more, God or yourself? Writing this book was not part of my plan. Thank goodness I am not following my plan. Why? Because if I did, there is no way I would have spent hundreds of hours of my time and money to write and publish this book for others.

Your spiritual gifts are not from you; they are from God, for God, and to be used to glorify God. We will talk later about how God's divine design includes selecting a vocation that aligns with God's divine design for your life. At the same time, we can all use our gifts to serve in our church, community, family, neighborhood, and workplace to do the work God calls us to do and to honor and glorify God.

Later, we will go into detail about how spiritual gifts operate.

4. *It will help me to help other believers and fulfill God's purpose.* I don't know about you, but I get fired up helping other believers and fulfilling God's purpose. When we live in alignment with how God designed us, we experience the gratification of helping other believers and fulfilling God's purpose for our lives.

When God called me to write this book, it was a huge leap of faith. There is no way I could have done it with my own power. What kept me going was that I wanted to obey God out of love for God and help people who didn't know their purpose, spiritual gifts, or God's divine design. As I began, the Lord revealed to me how He planted this seed in my heart years ago and how He orchestrated developing and using my spiritual gifts, talents, and abilities while teaching and coaching others to do the same to glorify God. As you reflect on God's goodness in your life, you will be in awe of how God's plan and purpose for your life prevails.

5. *It will help me reflect the character of God, receive the blessings of God, and learn how to be all God wants me to be!* God wants us to imitate Jesus, to be a light unto others, reflecting His character and the love of Christ. What do the people around you see when they interact with you? Do they see someone who is kind, patient, loving, gentle, and focused on and interested in helping others? If not, you may have some work to do. Jesus is our role model, for he lived in perfect alignment with God's will.

> For I have come down from heaven not to do my will but to do the will of him who sent me. (John 6:38 NIV)

When we nourish ourselves with the Word of God and by doing the will of God, we understand the character and will of God.

Jesus goes on to say in John 34–35 that the food that sustains us is doing the will of God to finish the work that was started. He tells us to open our eyes and look at the needs of those right in front of us. The harvest is plentiful.

This is a great time to stop and pray.

Prayer:

"Lord, help me understand the work You are doing in the world and give me a burden in my heart for the needs of others You place in my path. Guide me to discover and use my spiritual gifts, purpose, and all You have given me to serve others and satisfy those needs. Use me, Lord, to bless others and to glorify You today. In Jesus's name, I pray. Amen."

If we don't know and develop our spiritual gifts and align to God's divine design, how can we be nourished to do the will of God and finish the work of God? You can now see how important it is to discover, develop, and align your spiritual gifts, passion, purpose, and everything else you have been given to align to God's divine design.

As you grow your spiritual gifts, they become stronger. The Holy Spirit fills us up as we serve others to glorify God. When we become a vessel to bless others under the direction and love of the Holy Spirit, we continue to be filled up.

If you don't know your spiritual gifts or it's been a while since you took an assessment, you may be asking, "How can I discover my spiritual gifts?" There are many spiritual gift assessments available online.

Three simple steps to discover your spiritual gifts.

1. *Complete an assessment online by going to your church website.* If your church doesn't have a spiritual gift assessment, you can ask your pastor for the spiritual gift assessment your church recommends.

    If your church does not have a recommended spiritual gift assessment, you can use Google to search "spiritual gift assessments" online via churches in your area. Most assessments provide a list of the definitions of each gift.

2. *Print and review the definitions of your spiritual gifts and the list of gifts as you read the next chapter.* Keep in mind, the Bible does not give a specific definition of each spiritual gift; thus, don't limit yourself with one definition. Instead, study several different definitions, pray, and ask other believers in your small group or people who know you well for feedback on the definition that best applies to you.

3. *Talk to another believer about your spiritual gifts.* Whether it is a family member, a friend, or someone at your church, share with them what you learned. Sharing what you learn with someone else will help you ignite your God-given potential and align to God's divine design.

In the next section, we will review and explore spiritual gifts and how you can develop them.

Prayer:

"Father, thank You so much for what You have given me. Thank You for my spiritual gifts and abilities. Lord, I come to You with an open heart and desire to know You better and love You more. Thank You for teaching me about Your Word. I want to steward the gifts You gave me and glorify You in all I say, think, and do. Holy Spirit, reveal to me what You want me to know, say, and do as a result of reading this chapter. Direct my steps. In Jesus's name, I pray. Amen."

Discovery and Application Questions: Align to God's Divine Design and Ignite Your Potential!

- What did I learn?

- What does the Holy Spirit want me to do today?

- What can I apply or do to align to God's divine design?

Don't extinguish your potential! Instead, take action to ignite your God-given potential, serve others, and be all God designed you to be!

MILESTONE

Develop Your Spiritual Gifts

As you explore how you can develop and use your spiritual gifts, ask yourself the following questions:

- What are my spiritual gifts?
- Why do awareness, flexibility, and fit matter?
- How do spiritual gifts operate?
- How can I develop my spiritual gifts?
- What can I do to serve others with my gifts?

Now that you have completed your spiritual gift assessment and printed the definitions, we will explore what they mean and the link to God's divine design.

Why God's Divine Design?

You can start to complete your profile located at the end of milestone 5. Be sure to write down your spiritual gifts. Completing this profile will help you create visibility to God's divine design and understand what makes you unique and different. Why is that important? To steward your design to maximize the kingdom impact, bless others and honor God.

Your profile creates visibility to your unique design. This helps you leverage your assets and prioritize what matters most, and it serves as a filter to make good personal and career decisions.

Knowing God's divine design eliminates a lot of stress and helps you avoid going off road by making choices that don't align with your design. Did you know that up to 85 percent of people don't like their jobs? Why? They are mismatched. If you are in business, you've probably heard how important it is to get the right people into the right seats on the bus. If you match the right person to the wrong seat, meaning the wrong job, you cannot grow. It's both the employer's job and the employee's job to ensure the right fit. Don't wait for someone else to tell you how special and unique you are. Don't wait for someone else to determine the job that is the best fit for you. Whether you are starting your career, seeking a promotion, or experiencing a transition in your life, learning God's divine design for your life will help you make good choices to be the best version of yourself. Understanding your design will help align your strengths to get the right job fit. You will be most successful when you lead with and build upon your spiritual gifts, talents, abilities, and purpose. Completing your profile will give you visibility to your sweet spot that we will talk about in milestone 5, or chapter 5. Nobody else can do this for you. Take responsibility to steward what God has given you.

Most people I train and coach agree they need help gaining clarity. I share that with you so if you lack clarity, you will know you are not alone. Once they have clarity on their spiritual gifts, talents, abilities, passions, and purpose and God's divine design, they come alive. They go from critical juncture to confidence and become ignited! It is so cool to see them equipped and empowered to live a blessed life for God.

Personally, I discovered this in my walk with God. It was not in a class. There wasn't a book like this, so I wrote a chapter in my book *Ignite Your Selling Potential: 7 Simple Accelerators to Drive*

Revenue and Results Fast. In chapter 3, "Gain Clarity About Yourself, Your Role and Your Destination," I outlined the questions to ask to get into your sweet spot. This included questions about purpose, vision, spiritual gifts, and more. That's where you can make the greatest difference and ignite your potential. That book was a call from God to write in November 2013 and was published in 2015. Nearly everyone I trained shared the benefits of learning their spiritual gifts and purpose and God's design for their life because most people didn't know these things. People constantly told me, "This is far more than a sales book. It really applies to anyone who wants to ignite their potential." I agreed and promised, "My next book will be *Ignite Your Potential.*" Later, God revealed to me that my next book would be dedicated to God and talking about the greatness of our God. I share this story with you to show you that God has an amazing plan and purpose for your life, one you couldn't think up on your own.

The number one question people asked me after reading my first book was "What is a spiritual gift?" Keep in mind, this was a book on helping people sell more and become more! After failing to answer that question as well I wanted to, I prayed, and the Holy Spirit led me to design and teach a course on spiritual gifts and how to align to God's divine design. As I researched and spent seven months designing the course, I had a big ah-ha moment and realized, *This is the story of my life. After all, God led me to discover, develop, and align my spiritual gifts to His divine design.*

I then invested three more years teaching, studying, and praying to God to reveal what He wanted me to do. Then He led me to write this book. Now I am in alignment with God's plan. You see, this book was a seed God planted in my heart before I could even articulate it. I didn't know that His plan was for me to teach a course and write this book.

God has placed treasures to include seeds, gifts, abilities, and dreams inside of you!

Seeds start to grow in the dark before they break ground. You have seeds inside of you that want to grow. They need to be watered to sprout! The keys are to stay connected daily to God through prayer, study His Word, and obey God's direction every step of the way. God reveals His plans and purposes as we walk in a relationship with Him. God's Word waters those seeds. We have both an active and a passive role. The active role includes seeking to know God more, understand His Word, trust, and obey Him. The passive role is to receive His love and the blessings He wants to give you. When it comes to leadership, I think about how God created good leaders to be good followers. Following God's plan and direction is an aspect of leadership because God is the ultimate leader and will lead us when we let Him and are willing to follow. How do we find the desire to follow God's lead? We pray, surrender our hearts to God, and ask Him to help us become good followers of His Word and His will in our lives.

As I write this book, I am in awe of how God has a master plan and purpose for our lives. There is no way I could have anticipated how all these pieces fit together for His purpose and plan. The same applies for you. You have treasures inside of you, gifts, abilities, and dreams! Don't extinguish what God has put inside of you. Take a step of faith to discover, develop, and use what you have been given to bless others and glorify God.

I love the Bible verse that says, "'For my thoughts are not your thoughts, neither are your ways my ways,' declares the LORD. 'As the heavens are higher than the earth, so are my ways higher than your ways and my thoughts than your thoughts'" (Isaiah 55:8–9 NIV).

Now, when God asks me to do something I am not comfortable with or don't understand, I ask myself, "Who do you trust more? God or yourself?" The answer is always God. I have learned to keep God first. Trusting my plan above God's plan would be a mistake. God's ways are always higher than my ways. I say, "Yes, God!" and get going.

When I look back on the decisions, I made to follow God's plan, to trust God, and to say, "Yes, God!" I realize that they always led to success. I can't say the same when I followed my own plan. God's plan is always perfect. That doesn't mean it is easy, but it is the best plan because it comes from God.

What is God asking you to do? You can also ask, "What does God want to accomplish in me and through me to bless others? What needs has God placed before me?" If you don't have an answer to that, start reading God's Word in the Bible and pray for God to reveal His Word and His will to you.

Prayer:

"Father, thank You for the gifts You have blessed me with. I want to steward them well and develop them to build up and encourage people You put in my path. Show me how to use them to glorify You. Lord, reveal to me what You want me to know, say, and/or do as I read Your Word. I want to know You better, love You more, and align to Your divine design for my life. I say yes in advance to whatever You ask me to do. I know Your ways are higher than my ways. Help me to understand what You want to accomplish in me and through me to bless others. I want to keep You on the throne and honor You with my life. In Jesus's name, I pray. Amen."

Develop Your Spiritual Gifts—Three Categories of Spiritual Gifts

Let's look at what the Bible says about spiritual gifts in Romans 12:6–8, Ephesians 4:11, and 1 Corinthians 12:8–10. It can be broken down into three categories of spiritual gifts.

Remember, God uses all the gifts in each of these three categories to minister to His church and to accomplish His work in the world.

I encourage you to circle your spiritual gift(s) in this chart.

Motivational Gifts (Romans 12:6–8)	Ministry (Office) Gifts (Ephesians 4:11)	Manifestation Gifts of the Holy Spirit (1 Corinthians 12:6–11)
1. Prophesy	1. Apostle	1. Word of wisdom
2. Serving	2. Prophet	2. Word of knowledge
3. Teaching	3. Evangelist	3. Discerning of spirits
4. Exhortation (encouraging)	4. Pastor	4. Faith
5. Giving	5. Teacher	5. Gifts of healing
6. Leadership (administration or people focus)		6. Working of miracles
7. Mercy		7. Prophesy
		8. Tongues
		9. Interpretation of tongues

I've studied spiritual gifts for years, and I realized that not all books included these three categories. These categories provide additional clarity to ignite your God-given potential and unite with other believers to fulfill God's vision and mission.

As you learn about these three categories, ask yourself the following questions:

1. What are my gifts?
2. What is my primary motivational gift? In other words, what motivates me?
3. What do they mean?
4. What are the spiritual gifts of my family members, such as my spouse, parents, and children?
5. What spiritual gifts do my friends and coworkers have?

It is beautiful to see God's spiritual gifts in action in your family members, friends, and coworkers. I encourage you to focus not only on your spiritual gifts but also those of your family and the people around you. To help you do that, there are three things to keep in mind: awareness, flexibility, and fit.

Why are awareness, flexibility, and fit important? Awareness, flexibility, and fit are essential to honor God in others, stay humble, and recognize that all gifts, when developed and used under the direction of the Holy Spirit, are an expression of the Holy Spirit. Awareness of self and others and flexibility to tailor our approach to fit with other people's gift mix are key to honoring God in others, seeing people as God sees them, and igniting your potential. I believe it's important to take a holistic view and recognize our motivational gifts in all areas of our life. We bring our whole self to work, to church, to our families, and to our homes. Your gifts go with you wherever you go.

There is no good or bad gift. Everyone's gifts are valuable, just as you are valuable as a child of God. I say that because if you are not aware, flexible, and willing to tailor your approach when communicating or working with others, you can extinguish someone else's God-given potential. We build instant rapport with people who are like us and have the same gifts. It takes more effort with people who have different gifts. We want to value others' gifts as God values our gifts. We want to honor God by building others up and strengthening others. God designed us to complete one another and value the diversity of His family.

The apostle Paul identified seven motivational gifts, which are to be used in humble service in the body of Christ, God's church. When you discover and develop your spiritual gift(s) and use them to serve humbly and glorify God, you will experience joy. God designed you to experience joy and enthusiasm as you serve. No gift is better than another gift. Each gift and each believer are equally important to God's family, the church.

Do not compare your gift(s) with others; instead, embrace, develop, and use your gift(s) to serve those in need for the glory of God.

> For by the grace given me I say to every one of you:
> Do not think of yourself more highly than you ought,
> but rather think of yourself with sober judgment,
> in accordance with the faith God has distributed
> to each of you. For just as each of us has one
> body with many members, and these members
> do not all have the same function, so in Christ we,
> though many, form one body, and each member
> belongs to all the others. We have different gifts,
> according to the grace given to each of us. If your
> gift is prophesying, then prophesy in accordance
> with your faith; if it is serving, then serve; if it is
> teaching, then teach; if it is to encourage, then give
> encouragement; if it is giving, then give generously;
> if it is to lead, do it diligently; if it is to show mercy,
> do it cheerfully. (Romans 12:3–8 NIV)

As we review each category, let's also consider the application of each category.

Motivational Gifts

Motivational gifts motivate us to serve. They are to be used to build up, encourage, and comfort others and God's church. They will show up in all areas of our lives. When it comes to using your gifts, think of them holistically, to be used in all areas of your life.

Motivational gifts are key to understanding what motivates us and how God created us to help us serve Him more fully wherever we go. Knowing your spiritual gifts can also give you great insight into your vocation. If you have a gift of teaching, you will want to consider roles that let you use that gift to the fullest. If you have a gift of leadership, does the position you are in at work, or what you do at home or in your community, allow you to lead with your gift?

When a person accepts Christ, they receive at least one of seven motivational gifts: prophecy, serving, teaching, exhortation, giving, leading, or mercy. This gift of God's grace shapes how the believer views life, relates to others, and impacts the body of Christ. A motivational gift can be compared to how a person sees the needs of others and is motivated to help satisfy those needs. It also provides clarity as to their role in doing the Work of God in the body of Christ, God's church.

Prophesy

> Follow the way of love and eagerly desire the gifts of the Spirit, especially prophecy. (1 Corinthians 14:1 NIV)
>
> But he who prophesies speaks to the people for their strengthening, encouraging and comfort. (1 Corinthians 14:3 NIV)

Prophets speak truth and proclaim a message from God or principles from God. A more elaborate definition can be discovered via an assessment.

How about you? Do you have this gift of speaking truth and delivering a message from God?

_____

_____

_____

If you answered yes, explore ways to develop and use this gift in the church. Ask your pastor, "Who in the church needs encouragement and comfort?" You may decide to join a prayer team, whereby you can pray for and encourage people in your church or in the community with the Word of God and the promises of God. Look around at the people God puts in your path. Who needs encouragement?

Ask God to help you speak encouraging words and truth to those He puts in your path.

Serving

> For you, brethren, have been called to liberty; only do not use liberty as an opportunity for the flesh, but through love serve one another. (Galatians 5:13 NKJV)

A great role model with the gift of serving was Timothy, one of Paul's coworkers. If you have the gift of serving, you may be motivated to do hands-on work to meet the practical needs of others. People with the gift of serving love to help others. Paul knew he could ask Timothy for help and trust him to meet practical needs.

How about you? Do you love to help others and meet their needs in a practical way?

_____

_____

_____

If you answered yes, explore ways to develop and use this gift in the church. Where could your church use help to serve the needs of others in the church, in the community, or with church partners?

_____

_____

_____

There are so many places to serve in the church and with community partners. For example, Feed My Starving Children is a partner to many churches. We have a program called Blessings in a Backpack, whereby we can fill backpacks with food for children who are identified as food insecure. Then the nonprofit organization delivers the backpacks to the children at schools so when they go home over the weekend, they have food to eat.

As you complete your profile in the back of the book, you can identify the causes you are passionate about and areas you want to serve.

Teaching

> For this reason I have sent Timothy to you, who is my beloved and faithful son in the Lord, who will remind you of my ways in Christ, as I teach everywhere in every church. (1 Corinthians 4:17 NKJV)

People with the gift of teaching are motivated to pass on truth to the next generation. They will work to ensure the Word of God is taught accurately and that people's lives are transformed for the better by understanding the truth. They also care about the delivery of the truth. Luke was a great role model in the Bible for teaching.

How about you? Do you love to teach and help others learn and apply the truth for transformational results? If you answered yes, explore ways to develop and use this gift in the church.

_____

_____

_____

The more you use this gift, the better you get at teaching. One of the best ways to develop your gifts is by serving at church. Where could your church use your spiritual gift of teaching? In a small group, a class, outreach, one-on-one, or some other area? If you don't have this gift, what could you learn from someone with the gift of teaching?

Exhortation

> Beware, brethren, lest there be in any of you an evil heart of unbelief in departing from the living God; but exhort one another daily, while it is called "Today," lest any of you be hardened through the deceitfulness of sin. (Hebrews 3:12–13 NKJV)

The exhorter is motivated to encourage Christians to grow spiritually, avoid mistakes, and help people mature, discover, and develop their potential. People with this gift are great listeners and counselors. Paul was a great encourager. Jesus was the ultimate role model for all the spiritual gifts. He encouraged people to grow spiritually and to ignite their spiritual potential. Since our gifts are used under the direction of the Holy Spirit, it is the Holy Spirit who works through us as vessels to do the work of God. It is the Holy Spirit who ignites our potential and develops us to become like Christ. It is the Holy Spirit who carries out the transformation and changes lives. What a privilege it is to be a vessel and do the work of God, blessing others with our gifts!

How about you? Do you love to encourage others in their spiritual growth and avoid mistakes? If yes, explore ways to develop and use this gift in the church. Where could your church use wisdom, discernment, faith, or love to offer God's truth without judgment?

_____

_____

_____

If you are a new believer, you may find someone with this gift in your small group to provide great encouragement. If you are a mature believer, you may partner up with a new believer to encourage them as they develop an intimate relationship with God. You may also choose to explore leading a small group to encourage people to grow spiritually. Most churches need more small group leaders.

Giving

> Give, and it will be given to you: good measure, pressed down, shaken together, and running over will be put into your bosom. For with the same measure that you use, it will be measured back to you. (Luke 6:38 NKJV)

Matthew was a great role model for giving and giving out of love, as stated in the New Testament. This can include giving of our money, time, material possessions, or proper use or stewardship of the resources God gives us, such as our spiritual gifts, talents, and abilities. Examples include giving or helping meet the needs of others in secret so that it is done out of love, not to seek recognition.

God wants all of us to give and to give generously. If you have this gift, you may already be giving generously out of love and not calling attention to yourself. You may also be good at stewarding your resources so they grow and can be used to bless others. People with this gift can be a great asset to the finance team at church.

How about you? Do you love to give generously? If yes, explore ways to develop and use this gift in the church. If no, what could you learn from someone with the gift of giving?

_____

_____

_____

We can all learn from one another. I always admired people with the gift of giving. Seeing them give generously helped me become more generous. We are made to compliment and complete one another in God's family, His church body. Where could your church use the gift of giving to help others be generous? Where does your church need people to give of their time, money, possessions, talents, abilities, and gifts?

Leading

> A bishop then must be blameless, the husband of one wife, temperate, sober-minded, of good behavior, hospitable, able to teach. (1 Timothy 3:2 NKJV)

Examples of a leader who brought order into the early church was James. He had the ability to see the big picture. The Holy Spirit desires order. God is not a God of confusion but of order.

Leadership may include one or both types of leading: 1) administration, or organizing projects, details, and plans, then delegating with a task focus; or 2) leading with a people focus to inspire, create a vision, and motivate people.

People who have the gift of leadership and administration like to be organized and orderly and are task focused. You can count on them to get projects done on time and on budget.

Leaders with a people focus are gifted at inspiring, motivating, and leading people to achieve a common vision. They have the capacity to see what God is doing and how to bring about practical results to turn God's desires into a realty here on earth.

In the business world, leaders with a people focus are gifted at being vessels for God, sharing a vision, planning, and driving disciplined execution with transformational results. If you are in a leadership role in your church, community, or work, you will be most successful when you lead from your gifts.

How about you? If you have the gift of leadership, do you have a task focus or a people focus? If you have a people focus, you may benefit from working with someone who has a task focus, and vice versa, because you can complement each other.

_____

_____

_____

Explore ways to develop and use this gift in the church. Where does your church need either administrative leadership or people leadership? Examples may include leading a ministry, leading a small group, leading a project, or working alongside others to complement them with your gift of leadership, mentoring, or coaching someone. If no, what can you learn from someone with the gift of leadership?

Mercy

> Therefore, as the elect of God, holy and beloved, put on tender mercies, kindness, humility, meekness, longsuffering. (Colossians 3:12 NKJV)

People with the gift of mercy are tender-hearted and perceptive to the needs of others. They look for ways to be kind to others and love others unconditionally through the love of Christ. They desire to help those who are hurting. An example of someone in the Bible who had the gift of mercy was John. He cared deeply about the need for love in God's church, the body of Christ.

How about you? Do you have the gift of mercy? Explore ways to develop and use this gift in the church. Where does your church have people in need of compassion, kindness, and love? The same applies to your family, your neighborhood, your workplace, and your circle of influence. Who do you see hurting or in need that you can be kind to?

_____

_____

_____

Ministry opportunities may include healing and caring for people who are experiencing a loss spiritually, emotionally, relationally, financially, or other suffering in their life. Being kind, showing the love of Christ, listening, and caring for these people can be a great way to serve with your spiritual gifts.

Ministry Gifts

Let's talk about ministry gifts. God designed every believer to minister to meet the needs of others. These gifts bring order to the church but are not limited to pastors or staff. We need not rely on pastors to do all the work! Every believer can minister and contribute to building up, strengthening, and growing God's church family. Use these gifts as tools to build up God's church!

> And He Himself gave some to be apostles, some prophets, some evangelists, and some pastors and teachers. (Ephesians 4:11 NKJV)

Keep in mind that all gifts are empowered and enabled by the Holy Spirit.

Ministry or Office Gifts

- *Apostles*: Enable Christians to start new ministries and plant new churches where the Gospel has not been preached; may also include developing leaders and overseeing multiple ministries.
- *Prophets*: Receive revelation and speak powerful messages from God to people on earth.
- *Evangelists*: Receive the ability to clearly communicate the Gospel of Jesus Christ to others.
- *Pastors:* Preach and teach the Word of God and to take responsibility for the spiritual welfare of God's church body of believers.
- *Teachers:* Enable Christians to communicate and clarify the details and truths of God's Word for others to learn and grow spiritually.

While there are specific roles or offices within God's church for pastors and leaders, the church will not grow to its full potential if only staff members do the work of God. Ministry is not just for staff or 10–20 percent of volunteers. Ministry is meant to be done by the entire family of God, which is God's church. We can all use our gifts under the direction of the Holy Spirit to minister to others. God's church is designed to grow organically.

What percentage of the believers in your church are doing the work of God? If the answer is 10–20 percent, your church has a lot of unrealized potential. By igniting your potential and discovering, developing, and using your spiritual gifts according to God's purposes for your life, you can align with God's divine design and experience the joy of glorifying God by serving others.

What percentage of your immediate family knows their spiritual gifts and is serving at your church? What percentage are developing their gifts? How are you complementing one another with your gifts? How can you use your gifts in the community, in your sphere of influence, and in the workplace to help others and glorify God?

Review the list of ministry gifts and reflect by asking yourself, "What ministry gifts do I use to serve and meet the needs of others?" If developing and using your spiritual gifts is new to you, pray and ask God to help you develop and use your spiritual gifts to bless others.

Ministry and church leadership gifts are often confirmed when leaders and pastors join the leadership team. It's important to recruit a diverse team because all gifts are needed among the church leadership. Apostle Paul told Timothy, "Do not neglect the gift that is in you, which was given to you by prophecy with the laying on of the hands of the eldership" (1 Timothy 4:14 NKJV).

Manifestations

Manifestation gifts demonstrate how God works through a believer in specific situations with the supernatural power of the Holy

Spirit. Keep in mind, all spiritual gifts are used under the direction of the Holy Spirit. We are stewards of the gifts and vessels or channels for God. It is the Holy Spirit who puts His *super* power on our natural power. It is His supernatural power that transforms lives and brings healing, truth, miracles, and life to those in need.

Spiritual gifts flow out of the love of Christ when we make ourselves available to be used by God to serve and bless others under the direction of the Holy Spirit to demonstrate His presence and power to glorify God.

> Now about the gifts of the Spirit, brothers and sisters, I do not want you to be uninformed. You know that when you were pagans, somehow or other you were influenced and led astray to mute idols. Therefore I want you to know that no one who is speaking by the Spirit of God says, "Jesus be cursed," and no one can say, "Jesus is Lord," except by the Holy Spirit. There are different kinds of gifts, but the same Spirit distributes them. There are different kinds of service, but the same Lord. There are different kinds of working, but in all of them and in everyone it is the same God at work.

Now to each one the manifestation of the Spirit is given for the common good. To one there is given through the Spirit a message of wisdom, to another a message of knowledge by means of the same Spirit, to another faith by the same Spirit, to another gifts of healing by that one Spirit, to another miraculous powers, to another prophecy, to another distinguishing between spirits, to another speaking in different kinds of tongues, and to still another the interpretation of tongues. All these are the work of one and the same Spirit, and he distributes them to each one, just as he determines. (1 Corinthians 12:1–7 NIV)

As you can see, the Holy Spirit gives us these gifts. The gifts don't belong to us; they belong to God and flow through us via the direction of the Holy Spirit and are used by believers to serve others, build up God's church, and minister to others in need. God knows our every need. As we make ourselves available to serve others and be used by God, the Holy Spirit directs us to those in need. God orchestrates all of this through us and out of love for you and all His children! It's amazing!

Manifestation Gifts of the Holy Spirit
(1 Corinthians 12:6–11 NKJV)

- *Word of wisdom:* Receive supernatural understanding of God's Word and the will to apply it situationally in life.
- *Word of knowledge:* Bring about understanding and to inform the church or individuals.
- *Faith:* Encourage and build up the church's confidence in God.
- *Healing:* Speak life and healing, revealing God's Word and will to the sick.
- *Miracles:* Reveal the presence and glory of God to the church to create a sense of awe, wonder, and reverence for God.
- *Prophecy:* Receive revelation and speak powerful messages from God to people on earth.
- *Tongues:* Glorify God with the help of an interpreter to edify the church.
- *Interpretation of tongues:* Interpret the messages of God to edify the church.

To one there is given through the Spirit a message of wisdom, to another a message of knowledge by means of the same Spirit, to another faith by the same Spirit, to another gifts of healing by that one Spirit, to another miraculous powers, to another prophecy, to another distinguishing between spirits, to another speaking in different kinds of tongues, and to still another the interpretation of tongues. (1 Corinthians 12:8–10 NIV)

The Bible does not provide a thorough definition of each gift; instead, they are mentioned in multiple passages. To gain a thorough understanding of each gift, I suggest you take two online assessments; many are available via church websites at no charge. Then print the definitions and pray. Here is a prayer to get you started.

> Prayer:
>
> "Lord, thank You for giving me the spiritual gift(s) of _____. I commit to developing and using it/them to bless others and glorify You, Lord. Holy Spirit, direct my steps. Put people in my path for me to bless. Help me respond to Your prompting to love people like You do and to make myself available to help them. Holy Spirit, reveal to me what You want me to do. Direct me to the area of service in our church to advance Your kingdom. In Jesus's name, I pray. Amen."

This is such a powerful prayer. That was one of the best things a pastor ever told us at the end of a sermon: "Go home and pray. Ask the Holy Spirit to tell you what He wants you to do." It's a question I ask frequently. Every time God uses me to help someone else, I am in awe. It's such a privilege to be used as a vessel to help others and glorify God. You are designed to be a vessel too! God wants to use you to bless and help others every day!

You know my story. When I prayed that prayer, the Holy Spirit told me to talk to my pastor, who directed me to another pastor in our church. That pastor asked me to design and teach a course on everything in this book to the entire church. The rest is history.

> But the Helper, the Holy Spirit, whom the Father will send in My name, He will teach you all things, and

> bring to your remembrance all things that I said to
> you. (John 14:26 NKJV)

One of my gifts is teaching. I spent many weekends creating teaching materials, like this book, to help others and honor God. My small group at church confirmed leadership and teaching are gifts I excel at. The same applies to you. Once you develop your spiritual gift and start serving in the church, other believers will confirm serving with your gift is adding value to their life. It is by serving with your gifts and God-given design that you discover the treasure God placed inside of you.

But knowing I had the gifts was not enough. The workplace needs skills. Besides, God wants us to be the best at what we do. You can ignite your potential for God's glory when you develop your gifts. After learning I had the spiritual gifts of teaching and leadership, I got my master's degree in the areas of adult learning, training, and leadership, which is my primary motivational gift. That complemented my gift of exhortation to help individuals, teams, and organizations grow. I specialized in not only individual and team leadership but also organizational leadership to help organizations grow. By taking on additional responsibility in the workplace, helping CEOs, and doing executive coaching for twenty years, I developed this gift to scale organizations. This book has really been designed using all three of my spiritual gifts—leadership, teaching, and exhortation—to help you, your family, and God's family, His church, grow. That wasn't my plan, but it was God's plan. God's plan is better than our plan. God's plan and purpose always prevail!

God has a plan for you too. Develop your gifts so you can excel at using them to help others and serve God. When God wants something done, He first looks for believers who have developed their spiritual gifts, hearts aligned with God's heart, and those who are available to serve. I challenge you to get ready and make yourself available. God wants to have a personal relationship with you. He wants you to experience living a life in alignment with His

Word and His will. It's a better life than anything you have ever experienced. Being a Christian is not about religion; it's about having a personal relationship with the God who created you, loves you, and wants the best for you.

Your Spiritual Gifts

What are your spiritual gifts? Write them here. You may have one primary gift and then a secondary or tertiary gift. List your top three gifts from your assessment.

_____

_____

_____

Write down the name of a family member or friend.

_____

What are their spiritual gifts?

_____

_____

_____

What do your spiritual gifts mean? Study the definition of each of your gifts. There are many different spiritual gift assessments. Some have in-depth definitions, and others offer brief descriptions of each gift. I encourage you to look at several different definitions because the Bible does not describe each gift in detail. I suggest that you review your spiritual gifts, read what the Bible says about the gifts, share them with believers, and pray to ask God to give you clarity on what best describes your gifts. Don't limit yourself to one definition.

It is also beneficial to become aware of the spiritual gifts of others in your life, such as your spouse, parents, siblings, and close friends. Doing so enables you to encourage others to be all God designed them to be.

For example, you may have children who are highly motivated in a class or sports, but later in their life, they struggle to find motivation. You may have a daughter who was motivated in music, yet she struggles to figure out what she wants to major in during college or what career path to choose. Helping her to know her motivational gift and align her major and career with her gifts can help her overcome that struggle. Many people struggle with clarity. I often see people choose a career that doesn't match their gifts. This leaves them dissatisfied and at a loss for which way to turn. Many struggles can be overcome, and decisions can be made easier by understanding one's spiritual gifts and God's divine design for one's life.

I have helped so many young people and professionals make better choices and find the best career fit by going through this process. I have even coached pastors on discovering their spiritual gifts and purpose. It changed the trajectory of their lives, just like God used my spiritual gifts to change the trajectory of my life and career. Do the work; it pays off for the rest of your life and for the benefit of those around you! You bless others when you get into your sweet spot for maximum impact and contribution to God's kingdom. You will also be much more pleasant to be around.

Awareness, Flexibility, and Fit

In life and in the workplace, you need awareness, flexibility, and fit.

Awareness

Awareness starts with knowing yourself and knowing others' spiritual gifts. This helps you be sensitive to their style, what motivates them, and how they approach situations. You may discover that your spouse has spiritual gifts that are the opposite of yours. God may also put people with the opposite gift in your path to strengthen your gift or to complete you. Instead of thinking your gift is best, be humble and embrace the diverse gifts in others. Look at it from God's perspective. Everyone God created is God's masterpiece, full of God-given potential. It is beautiful to see how God puts us in a family and in His family with complementary spiritual gifts to complete one another. I am thankful that we are not all the same.

For example, one with the spiritual gifts of prophecy and wisdom could gain valuable insight and discernment from the Holy Spirit on what could go wrong in any given situation. This can be invaluable to troubleshooting, discerning potential problems, and avoiding hazards. Someone with the spiritual gift of faith may approach the same situation trustingly, believing it will go well and not seeing any of the potential problems. If these two did not know each other's gifts, they could extinguish one another's potential. Knowing one's own gifts and embracing other people's gifts enables us to be stronger together. We complete one another and embrace God's design, in which each person is valuable.

Flexibility

Being flexible to complement and complete other people's gifts is essential to building healthy relationships and working together in harmony. Let's not be arrogant and expect everyone to look at the world through our spiritual gifts. Let's humble ourselves, seek to understand others' gifts, and be flexible to relate to them as God designed and gifted them. Ignite and unite your potential with those around you.

Fit

Tailor your approach to the person you are communicating, serving, or working with. This applies to not only your spiritual gifts but also God's design, which includes your temperament or personality, plus your passions and purpose. Doing so will demonstrate that you value the other person, strengthen your relationship, and honor God.

> How good and pleasant it is when God's people live together in unity! (Psalm 133:1 NIV)

I call this awareness, flexibility, and fit. You need to know yourself, be aware of your own gifts and strengths, and be flexible to change not who you are but rather your approach, depending upon who you are working with. Tailor your approach to fit the other person's gifts, strengths, and approach. We are called to unity and maturity in the body of Christ.

> As a prisoner for the Lord, then, I urge you to live a life worthy of the calling you have received. Be completely humble and gentle; be patient, bearing with one another in love. Make every effort to keep the unity of the Spirit through the bond of peace. (Ephesians 4:1–3 NIV)

Remember, God does not make mistakes. Embrace His gift to you! When I was leading a small group and teaching on spiritual gifts, one woman had the gift of leadership with an administration focus. She didn't like the definition and wanted to change it. When asked why, she said she didn't want to be so focused on a task where she is insensitive to people. However, we are not to change the gifts God gives us; we need to embrace our gifts, as God's ways are always best. Instead, we can surround ourselves with people who have complementary gifts. We discussed how she can learn from people with the people-focused leadership gift. When you have the people—focused leadership gift, you care about the needs of your people above tasks. A person who has an administrative focused leadership gift can learn from or partner up with someone who has a people-focused leadership gift. A person who has a people focused leadership gift can partner up with or learn from someone with an administrative-focused leadership gift. That's a winning combination! Completing each other creates unity and increases your impact while honoring God.

God wants us to complete one another, not compete with one another. First, we need to be aware of and embrace what God has given us and how God has designed others who may approach things differently. He also wants us to see people through His perspective and value everyone as a child of God. I have seen so many people extinguish their own God-given potential and the potential of others. This creates unnecessary challenges downstream. We are designed to be compassionate to the needs of others and help others. Stepping into God's amazing design for your life is a choice.

Personally, I want to lift others up and be all God designed me to be out of love for God and love for people. I pray that you will ignite your God-given potential and the potential of others!

> But the manifestation of the Spirit is given to each
> one for the profit of all. (1 Corinthians 12:7 NKJV)

Validate and affirm your spiritual gifts, using them to serve and glorify God, knowing that is how God designed you. One person who was a teacher had the gift of teaching. An executive assistant had the gift of leadership with a focus on administration. Keep in mind, that may change based upon what God is calling you to do, because our career is not our calling. God cares more about who you become in alignment with His purpose, plan, and design for you than about a job or career. It's more about a relationship with God than a career selection; however, stewardship of your spiritual gifts overflows into all areas of your life. There is a bigger picture as to how you and I fit into God's epic story to fulfill His plan and purpose for our lives here on earth. We want to join God in doing His work until Christ returns.

How Do Spiritual Gifts Operate?

Why is that so important? To use our spiritual gifts most effectively, it's helpful to understand how they operate. Since God is our Creator and He gave us our spiritual gifts along with everything else, our spiritual gifts are designed to be used according to what He says in His Word, the Bible.

He already had a vision for your life before you were born. He had a very clear purpose and design for you based upon how He wanted you to function. He formed us to function according to His will and His design.

Only by understanding God's plan for how our spiritual gifts function can we develop our gifts according to His will and use them as He intended for us to use them. Let's look at how God designed spiritual gifts to function.

Where do our spiritual gifts function? God wants us to use our spiritual gifts to strengthen His church and do His work in the world. He gives believers a circle of influence. For some, that is the workplace; for others, it is the community; for others, it is our family or a combination of all of those. That was God's intent when He designed us and gave us our spiritual gifts. Keep in mind, the church body is designed to share the good news of the Gospel with the whole world. In no way do we want to limit where spiritual gifts are used because they go where believers go to do the work of God and serve others.

How do spiritual gifts operate? Let's look at five ways spiritual gifts operate.

1. *They operate in the church body.* God designed us to be part of His church body. A church is a group of baptized believers who have joined together in a commitment to help one another fulfill God's purposes for their lives. God designed each person to be unique and complete His

body. A church is not just in a building; it is a community of believers. As you know, the believers come from your community, neighborhood, workplace, school, and church community.

2. *They operate in the context of our values because values shape our behavior.*

Behaviors become your culture. What is a value? It's what you deem important. Values impact our identity and our success. Companies that create and integrate values into their culture outperform companies that don't by as much as quadruple! As Christians, our values come from God because our identity comes from our Creator. These values enable us to behave the way God designed us to behave! When our values and behaviors align with God's divine design, it helps us be all God designed us to be.

When I work with, coach, and train leaders, I talk about the importance of integrating values into their conversations daily and weekly. As a people leader of multiple teams, I carried our values with me everywhere I went, talked about them in every team meeting, and recognized people for modeling these values. This created a positive winning culture and helped us strive for excellence, which is God's will. God wants us to be the best at what we do for His glory.

> Finally, brothers and sisters, whatever is true, whatever is noble, whatever is right, whatever is pure, whatever is lovely, whatever is admirable—if anything is excellent or praiseworthy—think about such things. (Philippians 4:8 NIV)

Why? If you don't shape the culture, it will resort to the lowest common denominator. We have all been in cultures where the leader did not build a positive culture. When this happens, it inhibits growth and excellence. It doesn't have to be that way. If you are a leader of people in the workplace, your family, or a small group at church, be sure to create values and strive to live by them. People do what leaders do, not just say. I found that modeling values was as important as communicating them.

This is critical for small groups. People need to know what to expect. I create a code of conduct to ensure everyone knows what to expect and how to participate to not only grow spiritually but also encourage and support others.

I also share our kingdom values in our small group. As believers, we can all benefit from looking at kingdom values daily and aligning our thoughts and behaviors to God's design instead of our own.

Here are seven kingdom values that I believe are important:

- *God centered.* As believers, we live for God seeking to glorify God in all we say, think, and do.
- *Bible based.* We live in fellowship with believers seeking to be informed by the Bible, giving it authority over our lives.
- *Advancing the Kingdom of God.* We are motivated by the love of God, seeking to fulfil His vision and mission to make more disciples for Christ.
- *God reliant.* We humbly rely on God out of gratitude, faith, and expectation in prayer, believing His ways are higher than our ways and seeking His wisdom.
- *Follow Jesus.* We are followers of Jesus Christ, seeking to be transformed to become like Christ.
- *Stewardship.* We accept responsibility to use the gifts and resources that God has bestowed on us wisely for His glory.
- *Kindness.* Out of compassion and love, we seek to understand the needs of others and make ourselves available to be used by God to bless and serve people God puts in our path.

Why are kingdom values important? Kingdom values help us live in alignment with God's divine design for our life. As you read them, you can pray, "Lord, reveal what You want me to know, say, and do as a result of reading these kingdom values." Values shape our behavior. To shape our behavior to honor God, we need kingdom values. I encourage you to learn the values of your church. Living out those values builds unity in the body of your church. If you lead a small group, share kingdom values to build unity in your group.

If you don't already have your values written down, I highly encourage you to write them down and define them. This is also a great exercise to do as a family or a couple to ignite and unite the light of Christ in your daily life by shaping your behavior to be in alignment with God's divine design for your life. In the workplace, you can modify these values as needed. For example, in the workplace I talk about the importance of being humble and thinking of others. I train people to be kind, to seek to understand needs of others and to serve others. We can serve others by helping people to satisfy those needs. I recently did a search in the Bible for the word *kind* to discover it shows up 250 times! Do we need more kindness in the world today? Absolutely. Let's be the hands and feet of Jesus and be kind.

Once again, where is God's church? Not just in a building but in our family, neighborhood, work, community, and church. It can be where believers are meeting, in their home. Why is this so important? Because you will bear fruit when you use your spiritual gifts and everything God has given you to serve others wherever you go.

God designed every believer to do the work of God. This means it is not just ministers and pastors who serve. Every believer is equipped for works of service so the body of Christ, God's church, may be built up and strengthened to fulfill the Great Commission and the Great Commandment of bringing the Gospel and good news to everyone. God designed us to be successful when we do His work.

> And He Himself gave some to be apostles, some prophets, some evangelists, and some pastors and teachers, for the equipping of the saints for the work of ministry, for the edifying of the body of Christ, till we all come to the unity of the faith and of the knowledge of the Son of God, to a perfect man, to the measure of the stature of the fullness of Christ. (Ephesians 4:11–13 NKJV)

Serving in God's church matures us so we can bless others and become all God designed us to be. Serving ignites your God-given potential.

After I learned about my spiritual gifts, I talked with our pastors to explore all the service opportunities at church. We are fortunate that most opportunities are listed on the church website. God matured me as I used my gifts to build God's church and advance God's kingdom. That's how God matures us. He will mature you when you use your gifts to advance God's kingdom. Doing so honors God, and God rewards those who honor Him. When we use our gifts to strengthen God's family, people we serve are blessed, and God multiplies our impact. God's church was designed to be multiplied by each person doing the work of God. I believe churches need everyone engaged in discovering, developing, and using their gifts in the church body to strengthen and grow the church. As believers, we need to strengthen one another so we can use our spirituals gifts to advance the Kingdom of God. God wants us to be strengthened as a church body. He wants us to build one another up. He also wants us to use our spiritual gifts in connection with and under the direction of the Holy Spirit, who declares God's work. Spiritual gifts show up in the Lord's work. They are not decided on or revealed by us.

Make serving at your church a priority. That may be during a weekend service, in a small group, on a mission trip, or by serving a ministry partner in the community or world. You strengthen your spiritual gifts and build confidence when you use them. Spiritual gifts are like power tools. I remember one weekend when we were tightening the hinges on our kitchen cabinets. Some were hard to access, so my husband went to the hardware store to buy a power screwdriver. It took some practice to learn how to use it because I had never used power tools before. The same is true for our spiritual gifts. They are power tools. The Holy Spirit provides the supernatural power! When His power flows through you to bless others, you will stand in awe. The more you practice using your spiritual gifts, the more comfortable and confident you will become.

Do spiritual gifts operate outside the walls of the church? Yes, of course they do. They go with you where you go. Your spiritual gifts go with you to the gym, to work, to get together with friends, and to talk with family members. They go everywhere you go. You were designed to be the light of Christ in a dark world. Make serving God's family, His church, the body of Christ, a priority. There, you will join with a family of believers serving together. God needs more workers to strengthen His church and advance the His kingdom. That is not a nice thing to have but rather a need.

Secondly, know that when you help others and serve wherever you go, you are a channel or vessel for God's grace. You will find it will nourish your soul when you serve. It is far more enjoyable to give than receive. I believe the most successful people are givers, not takers. Be a giver to glorify God, who gave you everything.

Let's continue walking through how spiritual gifts operate.

3. *When we make ourselves available to be used by the Holy Spirit.*
   Since our spiritual gifts operate under the direction of the Holy Spirit, we need to make ourselves available to be used by God. This means we need to make helping others and honoring God a priority in our lives. If we don't create space in our busy schedules to serve, it won't happen.

I've always admired people who were generous. After doing some reflection, I recognized I had an opportunity to give more. When I saw people giving of their time and resources, I decided I wanted to become more generous. I prayed and asked God to help me become more generous. Next, I allocated 10 percent of my most valuable resource, my time, to give back and serve God's church. I took two thousand work hours per year and multiplied it by 10 percent, then allocated two hundred hours of volunteer time to give back and serve. When I broke this down quarterly, it was fifty hours a quarter divided by twelve weeks, or 4.1 hours a week. This may seem like a lot; however, when God gives us twenty-four hours a day, seven days a week, which is 8,736 hours per year, the least I can do is give back two hundred hours a year! Think about it. What if you watched one hour less of TV or spent one hour less on social media each day? If you multiply that by four days, you would easily be able to serve 4.1 hours a week. Don't ask how many hours you have; just commit to serving a certain amount, and the rest will take care of itself. If I asked myself how much free time I had to give back, the answer would have been zero. We make time once we commit.

Next, I prayed: "Holy Spirit, direct my steps. Help me to see what You are doing and to partner with You. Show me what You want me to do to strengthen and grow Your church for Your glory. In Jesus's name, I pray. Amen."

The Holy Spirit directs us when we make ourselves available and we ask. God is so loving that He does not barge in and make us serve. Instead, He invites us to choose to serve. Serving is a privilege. We don't *have* to serve; we *get* to serve.

God used me to serve in developing people by leading, teaching, and coaching. Whenever I serve, I experience the joy of being a vessel for our great God. As we discussed earlier, God always matures us spiritually as serve. Once we begin to serve, we develop a desire to serve more. That's what God wants. He encourages us to posture our hearts toward His purposes and

His ways. If we are vessels, we will never run out of love to serve. His living water will continue to flow through us.

When it comes to what we do to serve, we don't have to know all the answers. If we did, we would be relying on ourselves. God wants us to rely on Him. Simply ask God for help, and He will guide you. Sometimes the best prayer we can pray is "Lord, help. I don't know the way. Help me to know who You want me to serve today. Use me to glorify You. In Jesus's name, I pray. Amen."

God knows the needs of the His church body. I remember hearing a pastor say that every church receives the people who can complete the body of Christ and do the work of Christ that is needed in the church body. God also knows the needs of every person. God will put people in your path He designed for you to help. Every day, you can make a difference in someone's life and glorify God. For some, it may be taking time to listen; for others, it may be saying a kind word or offering encouragement; and for others, it may be doing something kind to help someone else. Get ready to bless others!

That's why it is so important for pastors and church leaders to understand spiritual gifts and have training along with a process that makes it easy for people to get involved, contribute, and serve. Taking a spiritual gift test is not enough. It is equally important that people understand what the Bible says about spiritual gifts, God's divine design, and their sweet spot so they can have the greatest impact to advance God's kingdom. Nearly everyone I talk with has a desire to serve. Why? Because God designed us that way. He knows we experience great joy when we serve, build up His church, and glorify Him. Doing so helps us ignite the light of Christ within us.

4. *They operate out of love.*
   The Holy Spirit pours out His love through us.

> Now hope does not disappoint, because the love of God has been poured out in our hearts by the Holy Spirit who was given to us. (Romans 5:5 NKJV)

It is the love of Christ that gives us the ability to be compassionate toward the needs of others and desire to help them. When you develop a relationship with God and get to know the character of God, who first loved us by sending His only Son to die so that we could have ever lasting life, you are able to love others. When people reject God and Jesus as their Savior, they don't have the capacity to love, because our capacity and ability to love comes from God loving us. Once we accept Jesus as our Savior, repent, and invite God in to be the Lord of our life, we are filled with the love of God, adopted into His family, and able to love others and do the work of God.

> For God so loved the world that He gave His only begotten Son, that whoever believes in Him should not perish but have everlasting life. (John 3:16 NIV)

Think back to a time when you saw someone in need and your heart prompted you to help that person. If you are a parent, it could have been when your child was sick, and you stayed up all night to care for and comfort your child. That is the Holy Spirit working through you as a believer to love your child.

How we respond indicates how we are used by God. We have all been in church and heard the pastor or staff share a need in the church or community, inviting people to respond. When the request is made, you may think, *I want to help. I want to serve.* That's the Holy Spirit working through you to have compassion, see the needs of others, and want to serve. Our response indicates how we are used by God. If we say yes, God uses us. If we say no, we miss out on that opportunity and the blessings that come with serving others for the glory of God.

Why is it that sometimes you feel prompting and don't act? For example, at the end of a church service, your pastor or a church leader may share some of the volunteer needs. You may feel prompted to help people in need or to serve, but as you walk out of church, you talk yourself out of it! The enemy tries to prevent God's children from doing the work of God. The enemy, Satan, comes to steal, kill, and destroy. This means that when you feel prompted out of love to serve others and honor God, but you talk yourself out of it, that is the work of the enemy trying to stop God's people from doing the work of God. Satan wants to prevent you from advancing God's kingdom and from experiencing the joy that comes with doing so. I share this so you don't fall into the enemy's trap. When you see someone in need and feel for them, act quickly to serve and help them. It may be an opportunity at church, a homeless person you see standing on the corner, a coworker, or someone in your neighborhood.

To avoid the enemy preventing you from doing the work of God, practice saying, "Yes, God!" and acting immediately. This may sound funny, but I proactively say, "Yes, God!" during my daily devotional time. Why? I want to do what God asks or prompts me to do. If I practice saying, "Yes, God!" I will be ready to say, "Yes, God," when asked. Don't miss out on the opportunity to serve. God will reward you eternally for doing so. Don't miss out on your rewards!

When we ask the Holy Spirit to reveal to us what He wants us to do and make ourselves available to be used by God, it's amazing what happens! You can be a vessel for God every day! There is nothing better than serving others and doing the work of God out of love.

For as long as I can remember, I have prayed, "Lord, use me to glorify You today." God would put someone in my path who needed encouragement, a listening ear, kindness, support, or help. I remember praying that prayer often. Then, at the end of a long day, a friend or family member would call me. God would work through me to bless them in some way. I had this happen nearly every day. I remember the first fifteen years of our marriage when I would talk to my husband on the way home or at dinner.

The first thing out of my mouth was always, "Guess what?" I was so excited to tell him about how great our God is and how He miraculously used me to bless someone that day.

One woman whose company I worked for reached out to me two years after she left. She was working for a new company. Out of the blue, she emailed me and said she wanted to get together after work for dinner. I didn't know why she wanted to get together, but I assumed she needed something. We chose a restaurant, and when we sat down to look at the menu, she said, "Get whatever you want; it's on me." I am not a big eater and don't believe in gluttony, so I ordered a salad. I asked her why she wanted to get together and what I could do to help her. She replied, "I just wanted to take you out to thank you for being so kind when we worked together. You asked about my husband, who was sick, and took time to listen to me. I could tell you really cared. I really appreciated that. It was a tough time, and I just needed encouragement."

I had no idea at the time that meant so much to her; however, I felt prompted out of love to listen, care for, and encourage her whenever I saw her. Sometimes you know when the love of Christ flows through you to help someone else. Other times, you may not see the result, but God always sees the fruit that He produces through us. Regardless of whether you see the fruit directly or not, I want to encourage you to make yourself available to be used and to let the love flow through you. Be kind to others and take time to help them.

You can bless someone every day by making yourself available to be used by God. By simply responding out of love to those in need, taking time to listen, speaking words of encouragement, praying for and with others, you can experience the joy of serving.

As I have matured spiritually under God's leadership, my prayers have changed. You may be wondering, *How can I get started?* Here is a simple prayer to help you:

Prayer:

"Holy Spirit, thank You for blessing me so I can bless others. Direct my steps today. Reveal to me what You are doing in the world today and what I can do to partner with You and bless the people You put in my path today. Give me the words and the prompting to be kind and compassionate toward whomever You send my way. I want to know You better, love You more, and serve You more, Lord. In Jesus's name, I pray. Amen."

5. *They operate out of the light of Christ.*

Then Jesus spoke to them again, saying, "I am the light of the world. He who follows Me shall not walk in darkness, but have the light of life." (John 8:12 NKJV)

Jesus modeled servant leadership, love, and light daily in every situation. Jesus was compassionate and acted out of light. He sought the Father's direction before He acted and was obedient to God's Word.

It is out of the light of Christ, the truth of God, that we serve and are to be the light of the world. When we follow Jesus, we can be the light in a dark world. Jesus came to this world to help the blind see and to save the lost. When we act out of the light of Christ, we are doing the work of God and honoring God. Walking in the light of Christ brings hope, joy, prosperity, wisdom, grace, and God's revelation to those who need it. Who has God put in your path that needs help? What does God want you to do bless that person today? Do it now! Take time to encourage the people around you.

When do spiritual gifts operate? When a person is born again. Spiritual gifts are given to every believer when they are born again, at their spiritual rebirth; they are available to be used as soon as you are born again.

Remember, spiritual gifts operate under the direction of the Holy Spirit. You don't have to be experienced in your own power to use them. The Holy Spirit will strengthen you with His supernatural power to do things you can't do on your own. We are vessels to let the Holy Spirit work through us.

The question is "Where does the wisdom come from, and where does the credit go?" I know where my wisdom comes from: it comes from above. Everything good that I have done or do always comes from God. God is the source of all good.

The wisdom comes from God, and all the credit goes to God. It is our job to keep God first, to seek His wisdom in His Word, and to stay connected to God daily in all situations. Let's give all credit for the good that flows from us to God, honoring God in all we say, think, and do.

> Where does the wisdom come from? Where does the credit go? The wisdom comes from God, and all the credit goes to God.

Let's walk through the seven purposes of spiritual gifts to gain more insight on how they operate.

Seven Purposes of Spiritual Gifts

1. Gifts are given to strengthen and build up the whole church.

   So it is with you. Since you are eager for gifts of the Spirit, try to excel in those that build up the church. (1 Corinthians 14:12 NIV)

To equip his people for works of service, so that the body of Christ may be built up (Ephesians 4:12 NIV)

2. Gifts are given for the profit of all.

    But the manifestation of the Spirit is given to each one for the profit of all: (1 Corinthians 2:7 NKJV)

3. Gifts are given to serve others, not ourselves. We are stewards of God's grace.

    Each of you should use whatever gift you have received to serve others, as faithful stewards of God's grace in its various forms. (1 Peter 4:10 NIV)

4. Gifts are given to glorify God and do His work.

    If anyone speaks, they should do so as one who speaks the very words of God. If anyone serves, they should do so with the strength God provides, so that in all things God may be praised through Jesus Christ. To him be the glory and the power for ever and ever. Amen. (1 Peter 4:11 NIV)

    For everything we have comes from God and is to be used for God.

5. Gifts are to be used to aid the church until Christ returns.

    That you were enriched in everything by Him in all utterance and all knowledge, even as the testimony of Christ was confirmed in you, so that you come short in no gift, eagerly waiting for the revelation of our Lord Jesus Christ. (1 Corinthians 1:5–7 NKJV)

6. Gifts are to be used under the direction of the Holy Spirit.

    But you will receive power when the Holy Spirit comes on you; and you will be my witnesses in Jerusalem, and in all

Judea and Samaria, and to the ends of the earth. The Holy Spirit gives believers supernatural power to do the work of God for the glory of God. (Acts 1:8 NIV)

Some consider the spiritual gifts to be power tools to do God's work because of the supernatural power of the Holy Spirit.

7. The church, God's family, exists to reach the world.

The Great Commission
Then Jesus came to them and said, "All authority in heaven and on earth has been given to me. Therefore go and make disciples of all nations, baptizing them in the name of the Father and of the Son and of the Holy Spirit, and teaching them to obey everything I have commanded you. And surely I am with you always, to the very end of the age." (Matthew 28:18–20 NIV)

The Great Commandment
Jesus replied: "'Love the Lord your God with all your heart and with all your soul and with all your mind.' This is the first and greatest commandment. And the second is like it: 'Love your neighbor as yourself.' All the Law and the Prophets hang on these two commandments." (Matthew 22:37–40 NIV)

Jesus calls all of us to be leaders and to serve. God did not design the church for pastors and staff to do all the work. There were times in my life when I was so busy with work and traveling that I let other things take priority and didn't make time to serve. That's not the case anymore. As God matured me spiritually, I made it a priority to serve and give back. I share that with you to encourage you to serve now. Don't wait; God needs you to use your spiritual gifts to serve today, this week, this month! Make time to do it now.

When I read this in Matthew 9:35, God created a sense of urgency in my heart to respond. Jesus is calling us to leadership by sharing that the workers are few!

> Jesus went through all the towns and villages, teaching in their synagogues, proclaiming the good news of the kingdom and healing every disease and sickness. When he saw the crowds, he had compassion on them, because they were harassed and helpless, like sheep without a shepherd. Then he said to his disciples, "The harvest is plentiful but the workers are few. Ask the Lord of the harvest, therefore, to send out workers into his harvest field." (Matthew 9:35–38 NIV)

Five Simple Steps to Develop and Use Your Spiritual Gifts

1. *Commit your spiritual gifts to God and God's family.*
   What does *commit* mean as a verb? The *Merriam-Webster Dictionary* says it means "to carry into action deliberately." Let's look at what the Bible says.

> Those who accepted his message were baptized, and about three thousand were added to their number that day. They devoted themselves to the apostles' teaching and to fellowship, to the breaking of bread and to prayer. Every day they continued to meet together in the temple courts. They broke bread in their homes and ate together with glad and sincere hearts. (Acts 2:41–42, 46 NIV)

My husband comes from a large family, and it's a lot of fun when we all get together.

When asked, "How was your weekend?" I often replied with how much fun we had getting together with family. People would say,

"I wish I had a big family." As a believer, you are part of God's family, which is the largest family in the world, 2.56 billion and growing. It's the largest family and church in the world. You can get together every week to worship God and be in fellowship with other believers.

According to Lifeway Research, not only is religion growing overall, but Christianity specifically is growing. With a 1.17 percent growth rate, almost 2.56 billion people will identify as a Christian by the middle of 2022. By 2050, that number is expected to top 3.33 billion.

Every now and then, I hear people say that they left the church. When I ask why, they usually tell me about a specific person or situation they experienced. The church is full of broken people, and we live in a dark world, so the people in the church are far from perfect. Seldom do we hear the benefits of being part of a church family. I believe we are so blessed in the United States to have the freedom to worship. When I talk with others who moved to the US, they tell me how much they love this country and how grateful they are to be able to worship God in public. I can't imagine what life would be like without God's church.

Let's look at ten benefits of belonging to a church family.

1. You learn your true identity (2 Corinthians 5:17).
2. You are supported by others (Ephesians 2:21–22).
3. You discover your unique value (Romans 12:4–5).
4. You receive protection (flock) (Psalm 100:3).
5. You become productive (John 15:1, 5).
6. You motivate one another to acts of love (Hebrews 10:24).
7. You encourage one another (Hebrews 10:25).
8. You grow up and mature spiritually (Hebrews 6:1).
9. You get to and learn to live life in victory (1 John 2:14).
10. You develop compassion to meet the needs of others (Mark 6:30–44).

As stated in Matthew 5:14–16 NIV, you are the light of the world!

> You are the light of the world. A town built on a hill
> cannot be hidden. Neither do people light a lamp
> and put it under a bowl. Instead they put it on its
> stand, and it gives light to everyone in the house.
> In the same way, let your light shine before others,
> that they may see your good deeds and glorify your
> Father in heaven. (Matthew 5:14–16)

If your church or the people in it are not perfect, don't let that cheat you out of the benefits and rewards belonging to a church family provides! We live in a broken world. People inside and outside the church are far from perfect. God wants to bless you and support you with a church family. He wants you to be protected and supported and learn your true identity in Christ, to mature spiritually, to be productive and bear fruit. This happens when you belong to a church family. At some point in your life, you are going to experience challenges and need extra support. The time to join a church family and develop relationships with other believers is before you need that support. Learn to grow, support others, discover God's purpose, receive protection, and become productive, sowing seeds out of love to honor God and bless others. You will be amazed at your harvest. We are not meant to go through life alone. When I meet people who are defeated, they are not part of a church family and are alone, without support. That's when the enemy gains ground to steal, kill, and destroy. Relationships fall apart, marriages are broken, health declines, and discouragement increases. Don't let that happen to you! God wants you to be well and blessed!

2. *Develop your spiritual gifts.*
   It's our job to cultivate spiritual maturity by growing spiritually. When we're children, we were immature; everything revolves around us. When we become teenagers, we have to grow up, mature, and start to think

of others. God wants us to become mature. That means we need to continually grow in our relationship with God and our understanding of who we are in Christ and who God is by studying His Word, seeking to know Him and love Him more. God wants to bless you and is waiting for you to spend time with Him.

> Therefore let us move beyond the elementary teachings about Christ and be taken forward to maturity. (Hebrews 6:1 NIV)

Instead of relying on others, such as pastors, to feed us, we need to learn to feed ourselves so we can increase our understanding, mature, and feed others. We have a responsibility to pass on what we learn to the next generation.

> In fact, though by this time you ought to be teachers, you need someone to teach you the elementary truths of God's word all over again. You need milk, not solid food! (Hebrews 5:12 NIV)

Just because you have spiritual gifts does not mean that you are automatically strong in them. While you have the supernatural power of the Holy Spirit, you can still bear more fruit by partnering with God and developing and using your gifts. When you invest in developing and using your spiritual gifts to bless others and honor God, this pleases God. That's being a good steward of what God gave you. It makes God smile when we use our gifts to serve others.

What are some strategies to develop your spiritual gifts?

a. *Study and affirm your gifts. Identify resources such as books you can read or courses and seminars you can take to develop your spiritual gifts.* As a church, you can put together a list of resources by gift so people can easily find them and build a development plan. As a leader or pastor, you can share resources to help others develop their gifts and incorporate an assessment into the new-member orientation.

This is something that really helped me develop my spiritual gifts. I remember when I took the assessment when we joined our church. They didn't have any classes on what the spiritual gifts meant. My learning came from my relationship with God, applying what I am sharing with you, and studying God's Word. When I discovered my gifts, I asked three questions: 1) If these are my gifts, what do they mean? 2) How can I develop them to add value to people? 3) How can I use them to glorify God? Thanks to the Holy Spirit's guidance, I started reading leadership books, got my master's degree with an emphasis in leadership and training, and later took a course at a Bible college to develop another gift. People who value themselves develop themselves. As a child of God, you are valuable. Develop your gift so you can be a light unto the world for Christ. Ignite the light of Christ in you! Unite with other believers to become all God designed you to be.

b. *Create development goals.* Setting development goals helps you take deliberate action to develop the gifts God gave you to add value to the lives of others and honor God. Did you know writing something down increases your probability of achieving it tenfold? It helps you be a good steward of what God has given you. The enemy wants to distract you and keep you from being all God designed you to be. Don't fall into that trap. Set goals and create action plans to help you stay focused on being a good steward of what God has given you to bless others and honor God.

c. *Practice using those gifts daily to serve others.* It is through practice and use that you learn how to be a vessel and let the Holy Spirit lead you. It also refines your gifts and develops skills needed in the workplace. By developing your gifts, you add value and set yourself apart by being excellent at what you do, making a significant contribution to your employer. You may not see the impact daily; however, if you continue to develop your gifts and practice using them, you will be amazed at the impact for the Kingdom of God. After twenty-eight years of developing my gifts, it is very intuitive for me to recognize others' needs, be led by the Holy Spirit, and act out of love to help other people. Not only that, but it's a lot of fun to serve. You will find that you'll enjoy using your gifts to serve others, and it will bear fruit. You will be productive and energized at the same time.

If you are a pastor or a leader at your church, you can help your congregation by having people share faith stories about how they used their spiritual gifts to serve people in need. Then your entire congregation can see the gifts at work.

You can also list volunteer opportunities in relation to spiritual gifts. The key is to train leaders so they can have conversations with people who want to serve and help them serve in their area of giftedness.

3. *Dedicate your gifts to God.*

And do not present your members as instruments of unrighteousness to sin, but present yourselves to God as being alive from the dead, and your members as instruments of righteousness to God. (Romans 6:13 NKJV)

Humble yourself and dedicate to the Lord every gift you have. When you dedicate your gifts to God, you also affirm them. I encourage you to affirm them not only in yourself but also in your children, spouse, family, and friends. Every time I speak, teach, or coach people on spiritual gifts, I hear things like "I don't have any gifts." That is simply not true! "I don't like my gift." Saying that is so destructive; it denies God's greatness and His workmanship in you. It extinguishes your God-given potential. Have you ever gone out of your way to buy a special gift for someone, only to discover they return it because they don't like it? We all have. Do you love to buy them another gift? Probably not. You may decide to just send money or a gift card because the receiver is never satisfied. What I am talking about is different from sending them a gift card to purchase something they will enjoy. How do you think it makes God feel when He gives you a special gift and you deny it or want to return it? Don't be ungrateful and extinguish your God-given potential! Instead, thank God for your spiritual gift, affirm it, and ask Him how to use it to serve others and glorify Him.

When people don't affirm their own gifts, they don't affirm others' gifts either. I have a gift of leadership that is people focused. That means that when I train leaders, sales teams, and organizations, I prepare in advance. Why? It helps me help people to get the most out of our time together. With my gift of leadership, I wake up every day thinking about how I can help others. Prior to starting my own business, I was preparing for a training session and invited a product manager to present. To ensure the people would benefit, I asked for the slides in advance. I remember my colleague, who didn't have the gift of leadership, saying, "You always like to plan so far in advance. I am not going to send you my slides in advance. I'll send them the morning of my presentation." What he was really saying was "I am not going to focus on the needs of others; I am going to focus on myself. I don't value your gift of leadership, the desire to be prepared and deliver value to others. I am busy, thus will get my slides to you when I feel like it, last minute." As you can imagine, his presentation did not deliver value to people. It was thrown together last minute and less than mediocre. Looking back at that situation, I laugh. He didn't have the gift of leadership and didn't have any desire to demonstrate flexibility to help people. By the way, that attitude and approach is not God honoring. Instead, affirm your gifts and the gifts of others.

How might you affirm someone's gift? What does it sound like to affirm spiritual gifts in others?

"You have the gift of _____. That is a great gift. You are so good at _____. It will be fun to see how God will use you and your gift(s) to help others and advance His kingdom."

Saying this will help you affirm God's gifts in others! It will also help ignite your God-given potential to be all God designed you to be.

4. *Distribute your gifts! You have something to contribute! Use them to serve and bless others!*

If you don't use them to serve, you lose them. It's just like your golf game or going to the gym. If you don't practice or work out consistently, you lose what you have gained. The more you use your gifts, the more effective you become at using them. You need to strengthen, develop, and grow every gift God has given you. There are many ways to use your gift through serving, studying, and continually learning from being in fellowship with other believers. It's fun using your gifts when you develop them.

As each one has received a gift, minister it to one another, as good stewards of the manifold grace of God. (1 Peter 4:10 NKJV)

When God gives you something, He will give you even more of it if you steward it well. When God can trust us with the little things, He gives us more. Keep giving and blessing others! Besides, God gave you the gift(s) to be used. Think back to a gift you gave someone. What do you want them to do with that gift? Do you want them to open it? The best part of giving someone a gift is when they open it and use it. That's what makes us smile.

What does it look like when we don't make time to serve? We start to fill that service time with all the other things that we feel will satisfy us, but they don't bring us the same joy as when we use our gifts to serve. As you demonstrate the love of God through gifts that He gives you, you will experience fulfillment and great joy. As you mature in your understanding of spiritual gifts and learn to be available as a vessel, allowing the Holy Spirit to work through your gifts, you can bear more fruit, be refreshed, and avoid spiritual exhaustion.

Remember, the church body relies on every believer to use our spiritual gifts to strengthen it. Imagine how much churches across the country would grow if everyone discovered and developed their gifts, then united to use their gifts to serve others and strengthen the church body. I believe churches would grow exponentially and increase their impact.

Opportunities have a shelf life. I hope you share my sense of urgency to act now! Why? To help others discover and develop their spiritual gifts to be all God designed them to be, for His purposes, to advance His kingdom.

Whether you are in a small group or with a friend or family member, I encourage you to pause today and say to someone you know is a believer, "You are gifted by God to advance His kingdom!"

Here is an example of a prayer to get you started.

Prayer:

"Lord, thank You for the spiritual gift(s) You have given me. Holy Spirit, direct my steps. Reveal to me who You want me to care for, pray for, and share my spiritual gifts with. Place the burdens in my heart to direct me to the people and place You want me to serve. Help me be a good steward of the gifts You gave me. I want to follow Your prompting and serve in the love and light of Christ. In Jesus's name, I pray. Amen."

Before we move on, I want you to make sure you know that you are gifted by God and fully equipped to do His work. Seeing yourself as God sees you will enable you to trust God more, ignite your potential, and be all God designed you to be!

So Christ himself gave the apostles, the prophets, the evangelists, the pastors and teachers, to equip his people for the works of service so that the body of Christ may be built up. (Ephesians 4:11–12 NIV)

Each of us has gifts that can be of service. Every gift is needed and important to God's church. We don't discover and develop our gifts on our own; instead, we do so through ministry in the body of Christ. Our spiritual gifts will never reach their full potential if we don't use them to strengthen and build up God's church.

Developing and using your spiritual gifts is an act of worship!

The Bible says that God designed us to be a living sacrifice and develop a lifestyle of worship.

> Therefore, I urge you, brothers and sisters, in view of God's mercy, to offer your bodies as a living sacrifice, holy and pleasing to God— this is your true and proper worship. Do not conform to the pattern of this world, but be transformed by the renewing of your mind. Then you will be able to test and approve what God's will is—his good, pleasing and perfect will. (Romans 12:1–2 NIV)

Once I became a new believer at age ten, I wanted to do God's will. Once I invited Jesus to be my Savior, repented of my sins, and invited God to be the Lord of my life, I knew I was living for God.

Even though I didn't grow up in a Christian home, I still knew my life was not my own. You don't have to understand it all. God transforms us through the power of His Word and the Holy Spirit He places inside of us.

5. *Reflect and evaluate.*
   Reflect and evaluate what worked well, what you learned, and what you want to continue doing or do differently in the future.

   - What worked well?
   - How did the Holy Spirit lead you?
   - How well did you respond to the Holy Spirit's prompting out of love to serve and help someone in need?
   - What impact did that make in their life?
   - What signs of fruit did you see in others' lives?
   - What did you learn?
   - What did you enjoy most?
   - What do you want to do differently?

- What service opportunities do you want to build upon?
- What is God calling you to do next?
- What gift or gifts do you want to develop next?

God wants you to work in the area you are passionate about. When you work in your giftedness for the glory of God to serve others within the church body, the community, or the workplace, you will feel energized and exhilarated. What you do becomes an expression of God in you, directed by the Holy Spirit. It won't feel like work. God made you and me that way.

By reflecting on what you learned and liked most, you will gain insight into where you can be serve in your giftedness in the future. For example, when we served communion, it was an honor and privilege; however, when I created a small group to help people grow spiritually and develop leaders, I was exhilarated. There is a big difference. You will be most successful and impactful when you serve in your area of giftedness.

I learned to say no to what is outside of my spiritual gifts and sweet spot. I learned to say, "Yes, God," to what lines up with the needs of the church, my spiritual gifts, and my purpose. Saying yes to alignment with how God designed me serves as a filter to determine where to serve. If you say yes to all the good opportunities, you won't have the time or energy to pursue the best opportunities. The enemy of best is good. There can be exceptions, such as if the church has a critical need. If God calls me to help outside of my spiritual gifts, of course I will help. However, that is an exception rather than a rule. There was a woman in my small group who was involved in extracurricular activities every night. She typically showed up to our group late and was always so exhausted. That's what happens when you don't prioritize. Once she gained insight into her spiritual gifts, purpose, and God's divine design, she said no to all the things that cluttered up her schedule and yes to stepping into her God-given purpose and design. She was relieved and energized! I want you to know that is possible for you!

The enemy of best is good. Good falls outside of your sweet spot.

How can you gain insight? As we finish this chapter, I encourage you to write out your testimony as to how you became a believer. Why is this important?

- It will help you reflect on and remember God's greatness in your life.
- You will learn from it, and your faith will be strengthened as a result.
- Your testimony will provide valuable insight into God's divine design and your purpose.
- God instructs us to write down what we learn.
- The Great Commission tells us what we need to do. Sharing our testimony is being obedient to and loving God with all our hearts. This love is expressed when we share our story or provide proof of how God has transformed our lives for the better! By sharing your testimony, others can be blessed.

What does the word *testimony* mean? The Hebrew word is *Aydooth,* which means "do it again with the same power and authority." Every time we speak or read a testimony, we are saying, "Lord, do it again, with the same power and authority."

Here are some questions to help you get started in writing your testimony.

1. What was your life like before you came to know Christ?
2. How did you realize you needed Christ in your life?
3. How did you commit your life to Christ?
4. What is your life like now with Jesus Christ? How has Jesus Christ transformed you?
5. What is God doing in your heart today?

The first time I wrote my testimony, I didn't have these questions to guide me. The second time I wrote it, I used them, and it made a difference. God gave me more insight and more revelation on how He has positively blessed my life and how He blesses everyone who accepts Jesus as their Savior, repents, and commits to making God the Lord of their life. What a great God we serve! He transforms us daily when we seek Him.

Don't take the shortcut and just speak your testimony. Writing always provides greater clarity. Besides, it is easy to forget how much God has really done in our lives if we don't write it down. By writing it out and saving it, you can look back at God's great work and His presence in your life. I am not asking you to do anything I have not done. God has shown me the value of writing out, and sharing my testimony.

During our small group, I asked people to share their written testimonies. It was amazing to hear how God came to the rescue, transforming each person for the better. My experience is that when people don't write it out, they are not prepared to share their story with someone else. Writing out your testimony is the first step to being prepared. Sharing it with others is an act of obedience that enables us to bless others.

Prayer:

"Heavenly Father, thank You so much for the gift(s) You have given me. Show me how I can steward them well to honor You. I want to be a doer of Your Word. Lord, I may not understand it all, but I want to say "Yes, God!" Direct my steps to develop and use my gifts to strengthen, grow, and advance Your kingdom. Lead me to use everything You have given me, including my testimony, to bless others and to glorify You. Reveal to me who You want me to pray for, care for, and share what I learn with. I pray that you send out workers into your harvest field. In Jesus's name, I pray. Amen."

Discovery and Application Questions: Align to God's Divine Design and Ignite Your Potential!

1. What did I learn?

2. What does the Holy Spirit want me to do today?

3. What can I apply or do to align to God's divine design?

Don't extinguish your potential! Take action to ignite your God-given potential, serve others, and be all God designed you to be.

MILESTONE

Discover and Align to God's Divine Design

In the first three chapters, we talked about how you were designed for significance by God, for God, and to do the work of God. That means God designed you to serve and make a difference in the lives of others.

You've learned how to discover, develop, and use your spiritual gifts along with why it is so important to do so. I also shared that nearly two-thirds of the self-identified Christian population who claim to have heard about spiritual gifts have not been able to accurately apply whatever they have heard or what the Bible teaches on the subject to their lives. In fact, congregations become spiritually impotent when members do not freely and responsibly allow the Holy Spirit to manifest God's ministry and power through the gifts He has given. Of all the times for believers and churches to align to God's divine design and manifest God's ministry and power in the world, the time is now. In a dark world, we need to be the light of Christ.

In this chapter, you will learn more about finding purpose and aligning to God's divine design, will, and direction, to be all God designed you to be.

What does it mean to live in the fullness of God's plan, purpose, and will for your life? It means aligning your life, what you think, say, and do, in agreement with God's Word, will plan, purpose, and design for your life. It's a better life living in alignment with God. God's will is always aligned with His Word. It means to live a lifestyle that honors God, based upon His Word and His will.

How? By being in relationship with God, seeking to know God more, trust God, and obey God. Once we become a Christian, God transforms us to be like Christ, which is what we discussed previously as part of God's sanctification process.

> Being confident of this, that he who began a good work in you will carry it on to completion. (Philippians 1:6 NIV)

This is my favorite section of this book because it is loaded with insight that, when applied, will help catapult you into alignment with God. My experience is that when I teach or coach and people discover their individual purposes, they come alive!

What's our road map? The Bible. Who is our guide? The Holy Spirit. Let's start with a prayer.

Prayer:

"Father, thank You for designing me for significance with a purpose, a plan, and Your divine design to fit into Your epic story. Thank You for the first gift of salvation and spiritual gifts to function under the direction of the Holy Spirit to build up and strengthen Your family, the church. I dedicate my gifts to you, Lord. I choose to walk in alignment, in agreement with You, Lord. Direct my steps and help me gain clarity on what Your purpose and plan for my life is. Remove any roadblocks that may hinder me. Shift me into complete alignment to use what I learn to glorify You and to advance Your kingdom. Use me to bless others. In Jesus's name, I pray. Amen."

Information doesn't change us, but revelation does. Revelation is information illuminated by the Spirit of God. Revelation changes how we think. Revelation changes the quality and trajectory of our lives.

When I was leading a small group, one of the questions I heard often was "How do you hear the voice of God?" That is a loaded question. The short answer to get you started is twofold: God speaks to us through His Word, the Bible. We need to open the Bible, read it, study it, and meditate on it to hear what God says. Remember, it is the living Word of God, so God will speak to you as you do this. Secondly, God speaks to us through the Holy Spirit, our helper, advocate, and guide. If we pray for the Holy Spirit to reveal Himself to us by giving us revelation before we read the Bible, He will do so.

If you don't understand the Bible, take a Bible-reading course. There are many available to learn how to read the Bible. Join a Bible-based church.

Why do I keep reinforcing the importance of application? Because the Bible says so and because I know when you apply what you learn, you will be blessed. I want you to be blessed!

But be doers of the word, and not hearers only, deceiving yourselves. For if anyone is a hearer of the word and not a doer, he is like a man observing his natural face in a mirror; for he observes himself, goes away, and immediately forgets what kind of

> man he was. But he who looks into the perfect law of liberty and continues in it, and is not a forgetful hearer but a doer of the work, this one will be blessed in what he does. (James 1:22–25 NKJV)

Keep in mind, we get the benefits of God's Word when we apply it. Understanding comes through application. When I read the Bible, I have my *Prayer Journal for Growth* and a stack of notecards to capture what God is saying to me and what He wants me to do. It's amazing to look back on my prayer journal and see how He spoke to me. I have learned to capture these revelations to see how God has and continues to work in my life.

As we continue this journey, I want to reiterate that the Bible is our road map for life. The Holy Spirit is our guide. This book is a road map to discovering, developing, and aligning to God's purpose, plan, and divine design to ignite your God-given potential. Instead of my opinion, it is a proven process of how God leads us to shift into alignment with His divine design when we are in a relationship with Him, seeking to know Him and love Him more.

Finding Purpose

Why is purpose so important? Because purpose guides and directs us. Without purpose, we lack direction, desire, and destination. Without God's purposes, we lack direction on how to live a life that honors God. Without purpose, people get discouraged, lose their way, and feel like they are not making progress in life or living up to their full potential. Without purpose, people extinguish their potential and miss out on God's blessings.

A life that honors God will protect you, restore you, bless you, and fulfill the plan and purpose God designed you for while you are here on this earth. Since we are all part of His story, it's critical that we understand His purpose for our lives, to be all God designed us to be. It doesn't matter where you are in life or how old you are. If you are a college student trying to figure out what to major in, an employee trying to decide if you are going to change jobs or pursue advancement, an executive working for a company, an entrepreneur growing your company, or retired, it is never too late to start finding your purpose. Finding your purpose helps you in all areas of your life. Without it, you will extinguish your God-given potential. Ignite your potential and align to God's divine design. You will be amazed at the difference it makes in your life, not to mention those you influence.

Your Progressive Purpose

What does progressive mean? It means it happens gradually, in stages, proceeding step by step. God revealed His purpose to us step by step. Sections of the Bible that were written later contain a fuller revelation of God than the earlier sections. God reveals His plan in stages.

We know from what the Bible says about salvation that our first purpose is to spend eternity with God. When we accept Jesus Christ as our Savior, repent of our sins, and invite God to be the Lord of our life, we receive the gift of eternal life, which is how God designed us. We become a child of God and are adopted into His family, His church body.

I like what Dr. David Jeremiah wrote in his *Turning Points Magazine & Devotional*, dated November 2021: "A Biblical View of Purpose referencing the Bible and Ken Boa's three tiered paradigm for talking about man's purpose: the ultimate purpose, universal purpose, and unique purpose of man.

Dr. David Jeremiah goes on to stay, "I'm going to use Boa's three-fold outline to jumpstart my own take on purpose, specifically how we can discover our purpose in Scriptures.[1]"

Below is a summary of what I learned.

Tier one is our permanent purpose, tier two is our progressive purpose, and tier three is our personal purpose."

1: Permanent Purpose

- Then I saw "a new heaven and a new earth", for the first heaven and the first earth had passed away, and there was no longer any sea. (Revelation 21:1 NIV)
- Our permanent purpose is to spend eternity with God in heaven. The world is not our home. Our first purpose with the gift of salvation is to spend eternity with God. I believe our permanent purpose reveals our destination.

2: Progressive Purpose

- Dr. David Jeremiah goes on to say, "But for the moment, we are here on earth, making progress toward our permanent purpose. God is gathering to Himself all those who dwell with Him for eternity. And that gathering place is called, the Church-the Body of Christ. (1 Corinthians 12–27; Ephesians 4:12). Paul makes it clear that our progressive purpose is to be a member, a participant in building up the Body of Christ. But our progressive purpose goes even deeper. God's progressive purpose in your life and mine is for us to be conformed to the image of Christ. Paul makes it clear in 1 Corinthians 12-14, that our progressive purpose is to be a member, a participant, in the building up of the Body of Christ."
- I learned that God uses everything in life for good, for those who love Him and are called according to His purpose. Our progressive purpose is not a destination, rather a journey in relationship with God. As we continue to seek to understand and apply God's Word and God's will, we are continually transformed. I believe the Bible and our relationship with God give us clear direction on how we are to live our lives according to His purposes.

"And we know that in all things God works for the good of those who love him, who have been called according to his purpose. For those God foreknew he also predestined to be conformed to the image of his Son, that he might be the firstborn among many brothers and sisters" (Romans 8:28–29 NIV).

To equip his people for works of service, so that the body of Christ may be built up (Ephesians 4:12 NIV).

3: Personal Purpose

- Dr. David Jeremiah says our personal purpose is to "glorify God and enjoy Him forever."

He agrees there is more. I believe God places desires in our heart that are linked to our personal purpose. As we seek to know, trust, and obey Him through developing a personal relationship with God, studying God's Word, and being in fellowship with other believers, we gain insight to His purpose and plan for our life. You will have an opportunity to discover your personal purpose of which I refer to as your individual purpose in the next chapter.

It's important to know that the world defines *purpose* differently from how God defines our purpose. What's the difference? The world defines purpose apart from the Bible and from God. Every January, when I go to the grocery store, the magazine racks are filled with articles on purpose. I typically pick them up and find that they say things like "Do what makes you happy." The problem is that these articles are all focused on serving yourself, not God. The definitions and directions are apart from God. When we define our purpose apart from God, who created us, it never works. This will not help you find joy and fulfillment in your life. It will not help you ignite your God-given potential and live life to the fullest.

The truth cannot set you free unless you know the truth. The truth is only found in God's Word and God's will! That is why it is so important to know God's purposes and be anchored in God's Word and God's instruction for our lives. Why? Because if we are anchored in God's purposes, we will not be led astray. If you want to know God's direction for your life, go directly to God's Word in the Bible and develop an intimate relationship with your Creator, God. Nobody reaches their full potential without an intimate relationship with God. Pray and ask Him for wisdom. Search for verses that reveal His purpose and His will for your life.

By contrast to the world, God defines our purpose in His Word, which is in the Bible. Where in the Bible? You can look at the scripture noted above for what I call purpose—permanent purpose, progressive purpose, and personal purpose, which is revealed by how God designed you and via your relationship with God. We will walk through steps to help you find your personal, also called individual purpose in milestone five. This is not to be used as a formula, rather to be used in relationship with God.

For additional purposes that link to our progressive purpose, let's look at God's five purposes, which come from two of the most important commands and are summarized in the Great Commandment and the Great Commission. These tell us how we should live in alignment with God's purposes.

> The Great Commandment: Jesus replied: "'Love the Lord your God with all your heart and with all your soul and with all your mind.' This is the first and greatest commandment. And the second is like it: 'Love your neighbor as yourself.' All the Law and the Prophets hang on these two commandments." (Matthew 22:37–40 NIV)

> The Great Commission: Jesus said, "All authority in heaven and on earth has been given to me.

Therefore, go and make disciples of all nations, baptizing them in the name of the Father and the Son and the Holy Spirit, and teaching them to obey everything I have commanded you. And surely I am with you always to the very end of the age." (Matthew 28:18–20 NIV)

In *The Purpose Driven Life*, Pastor Rick Warren suggests that these five purposes are worship, fellowship, discipleship, ministry, and witnessing and that they are derived from the Great Commandment (Matthew 22:37–40) and the Great Commission (Matthew 28:19–20). Pastor Warren writes that every church is driven by something. To understand each purpose fully, I recommend reading his book, *The Purpose Driven Life.* I believe these five purposes are essential to our role as Christians and being transformed into the image of Christ. When God shares these five purposes, He wants us to be in alignment with Him.

What does *alignment* mean? The dictionary definition is "to arrange in a straight line or a position of agreement." What does it mean to be in alignment with God? We discussed this in detail in a previous chapter; briefly, it means to position our hearts and lives around these five purposes. Alignment also means to agree with God.

This means to be in a relationship with God, in agreement with God's Word, and to obey God out of love. Jesus modeled these five purposes in His life, as noted in John 17. Our role is to position our hearts, thoughts, words, and actions so they are in alignment with these purposes that were practiced and modeled by Jesus.

How do you do that? Through studying God's Word, meditating on God's Word, praying, learning, being in a relationship with God, and applying it daily.

God gives us the Bible as spiritual food to know Him more. It's our role to seek God and to study His Word so we have clear direction and can align to God's divine design. If we don't know

His Word, how can we align? I have said it before and will say it again: the truth will set us free, if we know the truth. If you are not in a Bible-teaching church, get into one. If you don't know how to read the Bible, take a Bible study class or ask your pastors or someone at church for help. Many churches have apps that you can download that will walk you through how to study the Bible. These are great for when you are traveling or on the go. Many even have an audio setting that you can listen to.

You may be asking, "How can I get in alignment with God?"

Here are three simple steps that have helped me.

1. *Reflect on each purpose and ask, "How aligned am I?"*
   I prefer to ask God that question because His ways are higher than mine. Prayer: "Lord, on a scale of one to ten, one being low and ten being high, how aligned am I with You when it comes to _____? Reveal to me any areas I am out of alignment. Help me to shift into 100 percent alignment with You, Your Word, and Your purposes for my life. In Jesus's name, I pray. Amen."

2. *How aligned do I want to be ninety days from now?*
   If you don't have a strong desire to be in alignment with God, pray and ask for God to give you a strong desire to become aligned with His purposes and plan for your life. Prayer: "Father, thank You for Your wisdom and Your purposes. Ignite a desire in me to know You better, to love You more, and to be in alignment with Your Word, Your purposes, and Your plan for my life. In Jesus's name, I pray. Amen."

3. *Pray and ask God for help.*
   Prayer: "Lord, reveal to me how I can strengthen my alignment with You, Your Word, and Your will. I surrender my heart to Your truth and Your ways. I give Your Word authority over my life and want to be in full alignment with You, Lord. In Jesus's name, I pray. Amen."

My intent is not to teach on these five purposes but rather to share with you what I learned, along with practical strategies and tips that have helped me shift into alignment with God's Word and God's will. By no means have I mastered alignment; rather, I am still in process.

I've found that learning these five purposes and building them into my weekly agenda has helped me live them out. Prior to reading *The Purpose Driven Life*, every October, I prayed to God, asking Him to give me a word around which to build my strategic plan, both personal and professional, for the upcoming year. Throughout the year, I study what the Bible says about that word and pray about it so I can plan and live my life around that word. I have a list of the words He has given me every year for the past thirty years.

Why do I do that? Because I believe God knows our every need to fulfill our plan and the purposes that He designed us for. He knows our needs more than we do. God has the big picture and knows exactly what I need to do to shift into alignment with Him. Asking for His direction helps me adjust and align my life to His plan and His will.

Lessons Learned

Our first purpose is worship.

God is the source of all love. His love is unconditional. You never have to worry about earning His love; He always loves you. God's love is not dependent on your worthiness:

> For God so loved the world that he gave his one
> and only Son, that whoever believes in him shall
> not perish but have eternal life. (John 3:16 NIV)

In October 2021, God gave me the word *worship*. I have been amazed at all that He has taught me about worship this year. When we worship God, heaven comes to fight for us. When we worship God, He takes us to places we cannot go on our own. Since this book was a call from God to write, God knew far in advance that I could not do this on my own. I needed His wisdom, His direction, and the power of the Holy Spirit to write this. Our great God loves us so much that He gives us exactly what we need, when we need it. For example, why didn't He give me that word five years ago? Because I was not ready to write this book five years ago; I didn't have that need according to His plan five years ago. Instead of trying to chart my own course, I have learned to trust in God's direction, to stay in alignment with His plan and timing.

> "For My thoughts are not your thoughts, Nor are your ways My ways," says the LORD. "For as the heavens are higher than the earth, So are My ways higher than your ways, And My thoughts than your thoughts." (Isaiah 55: 8–9 NKJV)

I have learned that worship is not just about loving God; it is also about receiving God's love. When someone does not love God and receive God's love, they miss out on the fullness of His plan and blessing for their life. The only reason we can love others is because God first loves us. When we receive His love, we can then love others. God loves you too! He loves you so much He paid a price for you to be loved.

When it comes to loving God back, the Bible gives us a great example of a life that gives pleasure to God with Noah in Genesis 6:9. Noah consistently followed God's will and enjoyed a close relationship with him:

> Noah did everything just as God commanded him. (Genesis 6:22 NIV)

He was a pleasure to the Lord. Noah was in alignment with God.

During the global pandemic, I found that it was essential to lean into God. How do you find hope and peace when the world is in chaos? Intentionally increasing worship time with the following three actions is what helped me to experience peace in God.

1. *Increased prayer time and frequency.*
    Pray, "Lord, I receive Your love. Show me how to love You with my whole heart, mind, and soul. I want to know You better and love You more." God has helped me make some adjustments to be more aligned with Him. I pray more now than I ever have before. Despite circumstances, we can find peace and hope in God.

2. *Surrender.* Why? Because the heart of worship is surrender. I say, "Yes, God! I agree with You. I am in alignment with You." I say, "Yes, God!" daily before He even asks me to do something. That helps me say, "Yes, God," when He calls me to do something. I don't want to miss His request, so I find practicing this daily helps me act quickly in obedience when God asks me to do something. This postures my heart to respond right away to what God asks or tells me to do.

3. *Study, meditate, and speak God's Word. Declare God's promises.*

    > He who dwells in the shelter of the Most
    > High will rest in the shadow of the Almighty.
    > I will say of the LORD, "He is my refuge and
    > my fortress, my God, in whom I trust." ...
    > "Because he loves me," says the LORD,
    > "I will rescue him; I will protect him, for he
    > acknowledges my name." (Psalm 91 NIV)

    Since faith comes from hearing, and hearing by the Word of God, it is important to speak God's Word. Speaking God's Word moves it from head knowledge to heart knowledge, to understand and apply it. I want to encourage you to speak God's Word out loud.

> So then faith comes from hearing, and hearing
> by the word of God. (Romans 10:17 NKJV)

Our second purpose is fellowship.

God wants us to be in fellowship with other believers and encourage one another.

I have learned the importance of being involved in fellowship with God's family, other believers. Growing up, I didn't come from a Christian family. I was not exposed to church or fellowship with believers. As a result, I didn't know the importance of it. When I became a Christian, I always enjoyed going to church; however, being in a small group was not a top priority for me. While I took classes, I wasn't in a small group weekly. It wasn't until later in my life that I realized how important fellowship with other believers is.

I now make it a priority to participate in a small group and lead a small group to encourage others. I am amazed at what a difference it makes. It's fun to help others grow spiritually and be blessed by God. Looking back, I would encourage anyone to join a small group of believers. If you are traveling, there are multiple options available online. If you are not in a group, get into a small group. If you are not going to church weekly, join a Bible-based church in your area. Participating in fellowship with an effective leader helps you grow in alignment with God's purpose and plan for your life.

God designed us to be in a relationship with other believers to grow and support one another as we go through life together. The growth in small groups far exceeds what we learn on our own.

Another way we grow is when we experience problems and challenges. If you are experiencing challenges at work, at home, or in life, know that God can use this to develop your character to become Christlike.

When I am under pressure or experiencing a challenge, I don't always know how God wants me to grow spiritually. I have learned that I don't need to know how; all I need to do is ask God for help. I simply pray, "God, what are You wanting to teach me? What do You want me to know, say, or do in this situation? Lord, show me how to strengthen my relationship with You. I want to honor You and become who You designed me to be. In Jesus's name, I pray. Amen." God always responds and answers my prayers. When you ask, God will reveal Himself to you too.

I remember being on a team that God used to develop my character. I saw someone do something that was dishonest. It bothered me a lot, and I didn't want to have anything to do with that person. At the same time, I made a commitment and didn't feel that it was wise to leave this team. As I was driving from one meeting to another, I prayed, "God, show me how to love Your people." God instantly flooded me with peace. All the friction and anger about what that person was doing was gone. The next time I saw the person, I could sit next to him and love him. It was amazing. I still didn't approve of his behavior; however, I loved him anyway because God showed me how. You don't have to know how to do everything. God's power and presence is released in us when we share our weakness and ask for help.

Everything we do here on earth, can be utilized to develop us to fulfill God's purpose and plan. Heaven doesn't start once we die. It starts once we accept Jesus as our Savior. We are to bring heaven to earth by being Christlike and being a light unto the dark world. Our salvation is guaranteed; however, our reward is based on what we do with what God gives us.

Our third purpose is discipleship.

> "And teaching them to obey everything I have commanded you. And surely I am with you always, to the very end of the age." (Matthew 28:20 NIV)

God wants us to become like Christ and mature spiritually.

> For though by this time you ought to be teachers, you
> need someone to teach you again the first principles
> of the oracles of God; and you have come to need
> milk and not solid food. (Hebrews 5:12 NKJV)

When we are new Christians, we need others to feed us. As we grow and mature, we learn to feed ourselves. By the time we become adults, not by age but by spiritual maturity and growth in our relationship with God, we are to feed others. God wants us to pass on what we learn to bless others.

What does disciple mean? To become a follower of Jesus Christ, to continually learn and grow in how we can be a follower of Christ and share the good news with others.

Not all churches have a discipleship path to help people grow spiritually, which means you need to take ownership of your spiritual growth to be all God designed you to be. You need to intentionally pursue growth to be all God designed you to be. When you seek out God's truth, you will find it. Don't rely solely on your church to do this for you. There are so many courses offered via churches, Bible colleges, and online to learn God's Word and will. When you make it a priority to learn, seek, and grow, you will become more. You will value your growth when you are intentional and seek God. If you need help, ask God to help you.

I've learned that we need to make growing in our relationship with God a top priority. Don't rely on someone else to feed you spiritually. I am so thankful for all the pastors and people who have poured into me so I could grow. At the same time, going to church once a week is not enough nourishment for seven days. To grow, we really need to take time every morning to pray, study God's Word, meditate on it, and apply it. We can only give what we have. Growth enables us to mature so we have something to contribute to others. If the fuel tank is running on empty, you will find yourself seeking to fill your own tank and not be able to focus on helping others. It's your job to refuel daily. We don't get in the car without putting gas in the tank. Why would we want to start our day on an empty tank? Refuel first thing in the morning so you start the day with a full tank.

Mature believers refuel daily. As a result, they can think of and serve others. They are mature not only in God's Word and understanding of His Word but also in living in alignment with God's Word and God's will. They have an intimate relationship with God. Mature believers are givers. They have something to give because they have filled up on the goodness of God. As a result, they are filled with the joy of Christ. You can always tell when someone's heart is in alignment with God. They are full of the joy that comes from an intimate relationship with God.

How about you? On a scale of one to ten, one being low and ten being high, how mature are you spiritually? How aligned is your heart with God's heart? If you are at eight, nine, or ten, that means you are probably growing spiritually. You will experience great growth when your heart is aligned with God's heart and Word, and you are making yourself available to be used by God to serve others. If you are not intentionally growing in your relationship with God, you will not mature. When you don't grow spiritually, you won't have much to contribute to the lives of others. Be intentional in your spiritual growth. Seek to learn and grow every day so you have something to contribute to the lives of others. Investing in your growth and development to ignite your potential for His glory honors God. It is a sign of stewardship, using what He gave you to multiply His goodness in others.

We all go through different growth stages. Early on in my walk as a new believer, there was a stage in my life when I spent ten minutes at most in the morning for prayer and devotion. I didn't know the Bible then as much as I do today. As a result, I was ignorant of God's Word, truth, and blessings. I tried to depend upon God; however, I just didn't have enough of His Word and His truth in me. I felt undernourished, due to not consuming enough of God's Word. I am not proud of spending so little time with God. Thankfully, God pursued a stronger relationship with me, renewed my mind, and transformed my heart's desire to know Him more. As a result, I now spend more time knowing God and studying His Word and have made growing in my relationship with God a top priority in my life. Knowing God and loving God more has become a lifestyle. The foundation of knowing God is studying, meditating, and applying His Word, plus praying and worshipping God. Now I see others who need filling and want to help them become nourished with God's truth so they can experience the blessings God has for them. When we become filled up with knowing God and His Word, we can fill others up. That's how we make a difference in the lives of others and glorify God.

God designed you and me for a specific purpose. By growing in our relationship with God and other believers, we receive and give encouragement and support and mature spiritually.

In summary, find a small group at your church and enjoy the fellowship.

Our fourth purpose is ministry.

> Therefore go and make disciples of all nations, baptizing them in the name of the Father and of the Son and of the Holy Spirit. (Matthew 28:19 NIV)

> What shall I return to the LORD for all his goodness to me? (Psalm 116:12 NIV)

While our salvation is not linked to good works, we are called to do good works that God prepared for us.

> For we are God's handiwork, created in Christ Jesus to do good works, which God prepared in advance for us to do. (Ephesians 2:10 NIV)

I've learned to keep my eyes on Jesus and do what God says.

I learned the importance actively ministering to others, despite the type of work you do. Everyone can minster to others. You were designed to serve God, not yourself. Serving others is ministry. God wants us to serve others. How can you use your spiritual gifts and God's divine design, everything He has given you, to give back to God?

The world view is the oppositive of God's will. The world will tell you to serve yourself. Media will tell you, "Buy this product or this vacation or this car. If you do, you will be happy. You deserve it." Companies are spending millions of dollars every day to influence you to think you need their product or service. Did you know that in 2023, advertisers spent up to $7M for a thirty-second commercial during the Super Bowl? How many of you talked about the Super Bowl commercials? Nearly all of us have done that at some time. Whether it is consciously or subconsciously, those commercials are meticulously planned to influence you. And all that daily influence is focused on influencing you to be happy with something other than God. That same influence occurs 24-7 in the media and news. The ratings of the news station go up when people are afraid. The more they communicate fear, the higher the ratings.

The good news is that God did not design us to with a spirit of fear. Instead, the Spirit God gave us is of power, love and self-discipline. Love casts out all fear. He didn't design us to serve ourselves. Doing so will never satisfy us. Why? Because we were designed to be part of God's family, serve others, and glorify God. When we fall out of alignment with God's divine design, we will not find true joy. You will receive great joy when you serve God. It's important to know where true joy and fulfillment come from. Guard your mind and heart from the influences of the world and go to God's Word and God's will to find the truth.

I remember about twenty years ago thinking, *Why is it so hard to do the things that nourish us and fill us up? Could it be because the world doesn't reinforce doing the work of God?* At that time, I didn't know how to nourish myself with God's Word and God's will. It is a process. I want to encourage you to nourish yourself with God's Word and develop a personal relationship with God whereby you invest time daily to know God better and to love God more. Fill yourself up with the truth of God's Word and God's will so you can live the blessed life God designed you for.

Once you learn this, serve, and are involved with ministry, you will experience the nourishment to your soul and joy in your heart. Why do we give back? Out of gratitude to God and love for God. A great question to ask yourself is "What can I give back to God for the blessings He has poured out on me?" I spent hours writing this book. Why? Out of love for you as a child of God and out of love for God. I spent many Saturdays researching and writing this book. There is no way I would do that for myself. If it is in alignment with God's plan and purpose, then people will benefit. Blessing people who read this book and honoring God makes it all worthwhile.

I learned from Christian mentors to focus on adding value to the lives of others daily. Adding value, serving others, and ministry all mean the same thing. The key is to do it out of the love and compassion that flows from God, to meet the needs of others and be a vessel for the Holy Spirit to lead and direct us. As I shared earlier, every day, you can experience the wonder and joy of being used by God to bless others. The more you give, the more you will receive.

God loves it when we help others and are compassionate to the needs of others. One of our purposes is to incorporate ministry and serving into our daily lives. Some of you may be serving in your neighborhood, others in the workplace, others in your family, others in the church, others in a nonprofit or the community. You don't have to be a pastor to serve or minister. The work of the church, God's family, is not supposed to be done by only pastors and staff. God designed all believers to minister, add value, and serve the needs of others. God designed us to see a need and help others satisfy that need. That's one of the reasons I am so passionate about leading and selling: leading, selling, and serving are all about being compassionate toward others, seeing a need, and helping them satisfy it.

Not everyone who trains people to be an effective leader or sell has the same values. For me, leadership and selling comes from a very genuine place. I started leading and selling when I was five years old. After my first sale, I began building my sales team. I could see the needs of the people in my neighborhood: the need to have their driveway shoveled or the need to have their yard raked. I would inspire my friends to get off the couch and join me as we went door to door and asked our neighbors if we could help them by raking leaves or shoveling snow. It was so much fun! That was part of God's divine design, my spiritual gift of leadership and love for people, my heart to see a need, and my want to help people satisfy that need. That was a defining moment for me. When I became a people leader, I would always be on the lookout for what my people needed and how I could serve them and give them what they need to succeed. Not all leaders know how to serve their people. I can look back on my life and see how God's divine design allowed me to bless and serve others. God designed you with a heart to serve too! It's never too late to discover, develop, and align to God's purposes for your life. As Winston Churchill said, "We make a living by what we get, we make a life by what we give."

The fifth purpose is to witness, also called evangelism.

> Therefore go and make disciples of all nations, baptizing them in the name of the Father and of the Son and of the Holy Spirit. (Matthew 28:19 NIV)

> We are therefore Christ's ambassadors, as though God were making his appeal through us. We implore you on Christ's behalf: Be reconciled to God. (2 Corinthians 5:20 NIV)

How aligned are you with witnessing and sharing your faith? Have you written out your testimony, and are you prepared to share it with others?

One of the things God has taught me is to stay connected to the vine and be ready to share what God is doing in my life and the good news with others. It was not comfortable for me to share my faith with you in this book; however, I believe God wants us to share what we learn and what He is doing in our lives with others.

I don't intentionally try to have conversations about my faith; I simply spend time with God at the start of my day, study His Word, and ask Him to use me to glorify Him throughout the day. Seeking to know Him and love Him more and inviting the Holy Spirit to direct my steps to bless others for God's glory helps me to be a vessel.

One way we can be ready is to write out our testimony. When I teach people how to discover their spiritual gifts, find their purposes, and align to God's divine design, I ask people to write out their testimony and share it with the group. It is amazing to hear how God has come to the rescue of every person as they put their faith in God, repent, and accept Jesus Christ as their Savior. For some people, this was the first time they wrote out their testimony and shared it with others. It was amazing to see how God transforms every believer's life for the better! Writing out our testimonies prepares us to share what a great God we serve and how He can transform anyone's life for the better. People often say that writing out their testimony is one of their favorite sessions. Despite the mistakes someone has made, they are still valuable to God. God does not condemn anyone; instead, God sent His only Son to die on the cross so we could be forgiven of our sins and experience life everlasting. What an amazing gift of grace to share with those who are hurting, who are seeking, and who do not know what is like to be given a gift of salvation and eternal life that will forever change their lives for the better.

We all came to know God because someone else either shared their faith, witnessed to us, asked a question, invited us to church, or shared their testimony. I remember when I was ten years old, I was playing with a friend outside, and she asked me if I believed in God. I said, "Yes." Then I remember asking myself, "If I believe in God, why don't I go to church?" I walked down the street to this old stone church every week after that. The pastor looked like he was eighty years old, but every time I walked through the door, he had a big smile on his face. I can still see that smile today. Since my parents were not Christians, I had to wait to get baptized. As soon as I turned eighteen, I got baptized. I often marvel at how, if my friend hadn't asked me that question, I could have missed out on having a personal relationship with God and experiencing the greatness of our God. Something so simple can change someone's life for the better, just like it did for me. I learned the spiritual fruit of a Christian is other Christians. Reproduction and multiplication are signs of spiritual maturity and witnessing. That's how God designed us. To multiply and grow His church.

Today, I pray that I may use everything God blesses me with to bless others and that I am aligned with God's will and God's Word daily. I strive to be a river, not a reservoir. God blesses us to bless others. What about you? Are you ready? Have you written out your testimony and shared it with others? If not, I encourage you to do it now. Don't wait. You have an opportunity to make a difference in the lives of others.

Let's summarize our five purposes: worship, fellowship, disciple, ministry, witness.

What is our role? To position our hearts and lives to be in alignment with God's Word, purposes, and will. We should integrate these purposes into our everyday lives. It's not about perfection; it's about a relationship with our Creator and intentionally growing to know, love, and trust God more. By applying what He teaches us in our daily lives, we can progress to be all God designed us to be.

As a leader in your church, ignite the potential in your church to be all God designed your church to be. Revelation 3:1–6 describes a dead church, a church that goes through motions outwardly, busy with religious activity, yet lacks spiritual life and power. If your church is not teaching spiritual gifts, how to discover, develop, and use them to serve others and glorify God, it could fall into the trap of being busy, yet spiritually impotent.

How do the five purposes in the Great Commandment and the Great Commission line up with the five purposes of the first church? They are the same.

> Those who accepted his message were baptized, and about three thousand were added to their number that day. They devoted themselves to the apostles' teaching [discipleship] and to fellowship, to the breaking of bread and to prayer. Everyone was filled with awe at the many wonders and signs performed by the apostles [ministry]. All the believers were together and had everything in common. They sold property and possessions to give to anyone who had need. Every day they continued to meet together in the temple courts [worship]. They broke bread [fellowship] in their homes and ate together with glad and sincere hearts, praising God and enjoying the favor of all the people. And the Lord added to their number daily those who were being saved [witness]. (Acts 2:41–47 NIV)

Prayer:

"Holy Spirit, thank You for placing someone in my life to share their faith so I could put my faith in Jesus, confess that Jesus is my Lord, repent of my sins, ask for forgiveness, and commit to make Him the Lord of my life. Reveal to me where I need to rearrange my priorities to be in alignment with Your Word and Your will when it comes to witnessing and sharing my faith with others. Align my heart with Your heart, Lord. Help me to be ready to bless others, like You have blessed me. In Jesus's name, I pray. Amen."

Discovery and Discussion Questions: Align to God's Divine Design and Ignite Your Potential!

1. What did I learn?

2. What does the Holy Spirit want me to do today?

3. What can I apply or do to align to God's divine design?

Don't extinguish your potential! Take action to ignite your potential and be all God designed you to be. As a leader in your church, you may use this book as a resource to ignite the potential in your church to become all God designed your church to be.

MILESTONE

Your Sweet Spot

In this chapter, it is my intent that you will gain insight to your sweet spot and find your individual purpose. Let's start by talking about two words, *sweet spot*, that will help make a difference in the lives of others and steward what God has given you for maximum impact.

What is a sweet spot? It's an optimal place, point, or combination of factors that produces the best possible result with the least amount of effort.

When I was growing up, my favorite sport was tennis. In tennis, the sweet spot was the center of the racket, which produced the most power and control with the least amount of effort. I was the smallest person on the team, so I was looking for any help I could get to gain a competitive advantage. I learned that if I could hit the ball in the sweet spot, I would have a better chance of helping our team win the match. It worked!

In business, the sweet spot is a company's competitive advantage. Jim Collins, in his book *Good to Great,* helps organizations get into their sweet spot via the hedgehog concept by asking three questions:

1) What are you deeply passionate about?
2) What can you be the best in the world at?
3) What drives your economic engine?

These questions help companies identify what makes them unique. It is usually not just one thing but rather a combination of factors that catapult the organization to the next level. When you get the entire organization aligned to consistently perform in the sweet spot, you differentiate yourself from the competition and gain a competitive advantage.

When I work with organizations to help them grow, I help them discover their sweet spot and ignite their selling potential to serve their customers and become all they were designed to be. While there is more to their competitive advantage than those three questions, they always have greater impact and growth when I help them get into their sweet spot.

Going through the process of gaining clarity on your sweet spot provides insight, clarity, and visibility into how God designed you and what you can do to ignite your potential and be all God designed you to be.

In life, the sweet spot is where you experience alignment to God's Word and will, maximum work/life fulfillment and satisfaction, maximum impact for God's kingdom, and maximum contribution to bless others. It's about helping others solve unmet needs that God designed you to solve better than anyone else in the world. Isn't it amazing to think that God designed you to solve problems and help others better than anyone in the world? I stand in awe of God's amazing design!

Living in alignment with God's divine design is living the way God intended us to live. God's Word and God's will are our authority. It is about being restored by God into wholeness. It is about being the whole person God designed you to be. We bring our whole selves to whatever we do and everywhere we go. The Bible talks about integrity: our actions follow our words. We are the same person at work, at church, at home, and in the community. There is no inconsistency. I hope you can apply what you learn everywhere you go, with a focus on helping others and glorifying God.

Why is this so important? Because so many people don't know their spiritual gifts, purpose, and God's divine design for their life. You will never achieve your full potential if you don't discover your individual purpose. Furthermore, it will be difficult to make decisions without the clarity and direction that purpose provides. I see this all the time when I am coaching leaders who are not sure what direction to take their careers. They don't know if they should take a promotion or what they want to do with their lives and careers because they don't know God's design and lack clarity on their purpose. They have no understanding of their sweet spot to filter opportunities and make decisions. When they serve at church or in the community, they are not serving in their sweet spot, which leads to fatigue and burnout. I have measured workplace potential for over eight years. Many people are operating at 30 percent or 50 percent of their potential in the workplace. It doesn't have to be that way! God wants you to love what you do. God designed you with purpose. He designed you to be refreshed when you work and serve according to His design. When I say work, this applies to work inside the home and outside the home. It's not limited to people who have careers. Nobody ever achieves their full potential without helping others and glorifying God. In fact, it is God and the Holy Spirit who draw forth our potential. We don't do it through our own power. That's for sure.

God designed you to be unique, differentiated from everyone else. He wants you to know your unique design and to develop it and share it with others to advance God's kingdom. God designed you to satisfy a need in the world that nobody else can fill as part of God's epic story. Many people never take the time to discover God's divine design. As a result, they are not able to fulfill God's amazing plan and purpose for their life. They miss out on the deep satisfaction and joy that come with being all God designed them to be.

Once you gain clarity on your unique design and align it to God's plan and purpose for your life, you will ignite your potential and be able to be all God designed you to be. You will have clarity on how to make good choices that are in alignment with your sweet spot and design—choices on where you can serve and who you can help, along with the problems you help them solve to glorify God. It impacts serving at church, in the workplace, in your community, and in the world. Your work can also be a ministry when you help others and do it all for the glory of God.

When you align to God's divine design, the power and presence of the Holy Spirit in you flows out of you to add value to and bless others. The power source is God and the Holy Spirit in you. God put supernatural power inside of you.

To give you context, I learned about this more than twenty years ago with my relationship with God. He revealed His design as I sought His leadership in my life. When I published a previous book, *Ignite Your Selling Potential, 7 SIMPLE Accelerators to Drive Revenue and Results Fast,* I included spiritual gifts, questions, and steps to help sales organizations and leaders gain clarity on their sweet spot. Because it was a business book, I didn't share my faith or use scripture. The chapter on spiritual gifts was people's favorite chapter. Most people want the wholeness that comes from discovering and aligning to their God-given design. Wholeness and healing are part of the sanctification process God leads us through to be conformed into the image of Christ. God designed you and me to want to experience the wholeness that comes through our relationship with God.

My experience is that people just don't know how to get there on their own. When I see people struggling, the one question I have always asked myself is, "How can I help them?" In the workplace,

I don't share my faith openly unless someone asks. Since God inspired me to write this book and made it clear that I was going to share my faith, I am simply providing the background scriptures and sharing the inside story of the process. It is God who leads us to fulfill His plan and purposes and shows us the way, when we seek Him. There is no way I would have ever thought of writing this book and sharing my faith if God didn't lead me to do so. God wants to lead you too! To make this easy for you, I have designed a profile that will give you visibility to your sweet spot, which provides insight to God's divine design and finding your individual purpose. Let's walk through ten steps to find your individual purpose and ignite your God-given potential.

Ten Steps to Find Your Individual Purpose

Step 1: Spiritual Gifts

SWEET SPOT

What are your top three spiritual gifts?

Fill in the answers to these questions on your profile which can be found at end of this chapter.

> For as we have many members in one body, but all the members do not have the same function, so we, being many, are one body in Christ, and individually members of one another. Having then gifts differing according to the grace that is given to us, let us use them: if prophecy, let us prophesy in proportion to our faith. (Romans 12: 4–6 NKJV)

What can you do to develop them? Explore ways to learn about them and use them to serve God's church and bless others. How can you use them to add value to the lives of others?

Just because we have gifts doesn't mean they are well developed. For example, when I learned I had a leadership gift twenty-eight years ago, I asked, "What is leadership? How can I develop it to add value to the lives of others and glorify God?"

To develop it, I prayed and asked God for help. I read hundreds of books on leadership, completed a master's degree with an emphasis on two of my spiritual gifts—leadership and teaching— and then assumed multiple roles, both formal and informal, to use my spiritual gifts of leadership and teaching in the workplace. While it was a lot of work developing my gifts, it has been worth every sacrifice I made to go to school while I was working full-time and to give up some leisure activities to develop the gifts God gave me to serve others and glorify Him. I remember taking evening classes, getting home at 10:30 p.m., and reading or doing school projects every Saturday for two years. Any time you want to develop your gifts, there is a sacrifice to make. I share that with you to encourage you to make the sacrifice. The benefits of helping others and glorifying God are greater than the cost. It's well worth it.

It was by learning, developing, and using these gifts that I was able to add value to the lives of thousands of people and still do today. The workplace needs skills. Developing your spiritual gifts creates useful skills that help you serve others personally and professionally. I can't imagine what my life would have been like if our pastor had not implemented a simple spiritual assessment that he designed for us to take during our orientation class when we joined the church. If that is not the hand of God, I don't know what is! We serve such a great God! If this is new for you and you just discovered your spiritual gifts, add them to your profile. I will show you how you can set goals to start developing them and using them to serve others. You will be amazed at the cumulative effect five, ten, and twenty years from now. It's never too late. Don't think you missed out; start today!

Don't be surprised if a spiritual gifts changes, or if your desires change at various stages of your life. The Holy Spirit may give you a spiritual gift for a season based upon the work the church needs done. I remember my pastor asking me for help to develop leaders and to work on a new project for discipleship to help people grow spiritually. When I took my spiritual gift assessment again, I had the gift of apostleship. I didn't know what it meant but later learned it can be used in the church to launch new ministries. I am entrepreneurial, and I like to start and grow programs and businesses. God knew the new pastor needed help with that, so He gave me this gift for the season to help our pastor.

What is the difference between someone teaching who does not have the gift of teaching and someone teaching with the spiritual gift of teaching? The answer is transformation! Our spiritual gifts operate under the direction of the Holy Spirit. The power of the Holy Spirit flows through us to transform the lives of others. That's one of the reasons Jesus told His disciples that it was better for Him to go away—because He deposited the Holy Spirit in each of His believers, to be with us wherever we go. The Holy Spirit will transform people as you use your gift under the direction of the Holy Spirit to bless others and honor God.

As a believer, you have been given at least one gift, if not more. Make sure you develop and use your spiritual gifts.

Step 2: What Do You Love to Do?

SWEET SPOT

> Guard your heart, for it is the wellspring of life.
> (Proverbs 4:23 NIV)

God wants you to enjoy what you do, love what you do, and have fun doing what you do! Discovering and developing and your sweet spot and aligning to God's divine design to bless others helps you maximize your contribution to God's kingdom.

Enthusiasm is contagious. The closer you get to God, the more passionate you become.

What are you passionate about? What do you love to do? What gets you fired up?

When you pray for God to transform your heart's desires to be pleasing to Him, He will give you the desires of your heart. Check your desires with what the Bible says to make sure they are in alignment with God's Word and honor Him.

> Take delight in the Lord, and he will give you the
> desires of your heart. (Psalm 37:4 NIV)

Nobody else can do this for you. You need to tend to your flame and seek God to ignite your potential. He will perform His Word in you and through you if you ask Him. Keep asking!

> So I say to you: Ask and it will be given to you; seek
> and you will find; knock and the door will be opened
> to you. (Luke 11:9 NIV)

Some of the areas I struggled with the most became clear after five years of asking. Don't give up if you don't have clarity right now. Trust that God's timing is always best. I want to encourage you to stay the course. All the answers are in God's Word and in our relationship with God. As you work at seeking, you will find! Give God something to work with, such as studying His Word, praying, seeking, and obeying God to gain insight into what He has put inside of you and how He has designed you. Being a Christian is not passive. We need to put our faith to work, take action to seek God and God's truth, to align to God's divine design.

Make a list of all the things you love to do. Write it down!

Don't compare yourself to others or copy someone else's list. That will not help you. You are going to be most successful making the greatest contribution when you are yourself. The key is to be the best version of you! As you gain insight from God and God's Word, be sure to write down your answers on your profile. As you write them down and pray about them, you will gain more clarity.

Here is my example: I am passionate about inspiring, equipping, and empowering individuals, teams, and organizations to serve their customers and grow. When people are stuck or don't know the way, I love to help them. I have done this my entire life. It's fun. If individuals, teams, and organizations are not growing, they will not fulfill their potential and will experience a lot of problems, such as attrition, inconsistent revenue and results, and low productivity. Growth is critical to fulfilling their mission. The ability to consistently grow impacts the lives of everyone an organization serves.

Where do we grow? One place we grow is with other believers. God designed us to grow together, as part of God's family, which is the church. If you don't love God's church, I pray you will start loving God's church today. God's church is the bride of Christ. It is designed to grow organically via God's people. God designed you to grow spiritually, and a church grows when believers in the church grow and do the work of God. Discovering, developing, and aligning to God's divine design is all about growing yourself, growing others, and growing God's church. It's about igniting, mobilizing, and uniting all believers to do the work of God. Imagine if all believers were in alignment with God's divine design, doing the work of God to fulfill God's vision, mission, purpose, and plan. If we don't align to God's divine design, we will miss out on the joy of igniting and uniting to do the work of God, and we will not be able to fulfill God's vision, mission, purpose, and plan.

What makes you happy?

Another way to ask that question is, what does your heart yearn to do? My sister-in-law has the gift of hospitality. She loves to have people over for a meal. She is a great hostess. I love going to her house. Another sister-in-law loves to do projects. She is very creative and is always working on a house project. It's unbelievable what she's able to do. She serves her children by doing projects for them. That's fun for her.

I love to be with people and help people succeed. I love to study, learn, and teach by equipping people with things that help them overcome challenges and add value to their lives. I especially like to help leaders solve challenges at the organizational level and teach on leadership, sales, serving, and everything in this book. I love to speak, train, and coach people to navigate around their challenges and succeed. Helping people succeed and glorifying God by stewarding what He has given me to bless others makes me happy. I also enjoy creating teaching materials, courses, and books to help people succeed. I've had a list of books I want to write for as long as I can remember. For fun, I like to be outdoors and explore new places to run, hike, and bike. I am also an avid reader and love to read.

How about you? Write down the things you enjoy on your profile under, step 2. As we continue to grow ourselves with our hearts postured toward God, we have more to give.

What makes you cry?

Some of you may want to cry when you see homeless people or children who don't have food. Others may cry when you see people who are physically or mentally ill. Some people cry when they see marriages in distress.

Another way to ask this is, what burdens has God put in your heart? If the answer doesn't come to you right away, keep asking and pray that the Holy Spirit will reveal the burdens of your heart. Write down what comes to you. If you don't write it down, you may forget. Besides, the visibility of writing will help you gain clarity.

God will reveal the burdens to you. If you have not been aligned with God, don't worry; it's never too late. Don't ever give up. God will provide an open door for you to help others, providing you're open to His leading. Those burdens are important because they are linked to your individual purpose and what God calls you to do.

What makes you cry will be linked to your greatest pain.

Your greatest pain can be used to bless others. God uses everything for good. One woman had a burden for divorced women because she had been divorced and learned a lot about what it was like to raise children on her own. She knew she could encourage these women and save them a lot of heartache by sharing how God led her through her tough times.

Everyone has been through challenges in their lives and learned something in the process. Those lessons can be used to help others avoid the same heartaches or overcome challenges.

When you identify what makes you cry, ask "Why?" five times. You will learn a lot and can use that insight to gain clarity on your sweet spot.

God has placed a burden on your heart for something. It's your job to discover it with His help. This is linked to what makes you cry and your individual purpose. God has divinely designed you to solve problem(s) for others and honor God with your life.

What makes me cry is people who are stuck or feeling defeated, trying to go from here to there without clarity on where "there" is or are hitting roadblocks and in need of help. I remember taking a call on my cell all the way home from the airport one day. I was managing a sales team of 120 sales professionals and managers. As I walked in the door, I said to my husband, "My plate is full; I don't know why these people keep calling me for help."

He said, "Let's talk about that. Number one, they know you care; number two, they know they can trust you; and number three, they know you know how to help them." Since I led sales teams and business units to grow organizations, people came to me for help with leadership challenges and growth challenges. That is a sweet spot where I have spent most of my career. I didn't ask people to come to me; they just did. They sought after me to help them. People seek you out for help with something that God designed you for. Answering these questions will help you gain insight into what that is.

What burdens has God placed in your heart to help people with?

This is not just work related. My entire life, when I've seen people struggling, I have asked, "How can I help them?" It doesn't matter if it's an executive, colleague, or neighbor; the question I always ask is "How can I help you?" God gave me the gift of leadership to always know what to do to help others. It doesn't matter the challenge. Their challenge often becomes my burden. They may struggle with lack of clarity, not know how to achieve their desired results, need revenue, not know how to navigate through a tough situation, struggle with a decision, or be dissatisfied where they are and want or need help to change. Leaders often need a coach to work through tough situations, people issues, and marketplace issues. God gave me a heart to care about and help other people. My entire life has been focused on helping others succeed, helping others help themselves by making good choices.

It also makes me cry when leaders are stuck, lack clarity, or struggle with leadership, sales, or other issues that stifle their growth potential. Why? If they are not growing, they will experience problems such as attrition, limited growth, profitable revenue, or personal challenges. I have seen hundreds of people leave organizations because the leader was ineffective; the organization missed their goals and didn't know how to ignite their potential or the potential of their people to be all they were designed to be. That can be avoided.

If these leaders don't get help, they often stay stuck or go off-road into a ditch, taking people with them. The time to ask for help is before you need it. Successful leaders ask for help before they go off the road. Then I can help them avoid hazards and casualties along the way. I love helping people go from critical juncture to confidence to accomplish their desired results and ignite their potential. That's a burden God put in my heart. He equipped me to help them. I believe our world is at a critical juncture right now and needs the church to be the light of Christ in a dark world. It's time to ignite and unite as a body of believers. God placed a burden in my heart to help people who didn't know their spiritual gifts, what the Bible teaches about them, lacked purpose, visibility, and alignment to God's divine design. This book came from a burden God placed in my heart to ignite your God-given potential and help you be all God designed you to be.

How do you find this? One finds this through prayer, studying God's Word, reflecting on what problems people come to you to help them solve, and answering these questions. The root of your individual purpose is linked to what makes you cry and the burdens God places in your heart. Be sure to write these down on your profile.

What causes are you passionate about?

Are you passionate about feeding starving children, helping underprivileged children, literacy for children, education, the environment, getting homeless people off the streets, building orphanages, providing health care to the remote parts of the world, or some other cause?

One business executive was passionate about helping criminals turn their lives around, so he started a business to do just that. Another was passionate about transitioning family businesses to the next generation successfully. A friend of mine teaches English as a second language with her husband for people in the community through her church. Another friend enjoys reading books to children who don't have parents that can read. I met a couple whose parents experienced challenges as they aged and had dementia. They found it very difficult to navigate the health care system, so the couple started a business to help others navigate the health care system.

When you make yourself available to serve others and glorify God, He will place a burden in your heart linked to your passion. God placed a burden on my heart in 2014 to feed starving children. As a result, I donated my time and resources to feed one hundred million more children all around the world. It was very gratifying to see God use my gifts for multiplication to bless children and to advance His kingdom. That was linked to my passion to help organizations reach their growth potential to fulfill their mission. God gets all the credit, as everything I did was under His leadership. Now God has given me different causes to be passionate about. Causes can change, but your individual purpose remains the same.

Keep in mind, Spirit-inspired passions compel us to take action to help others for God's purposes. When you follow the promptings from the Holy Spirit, you will be fired up about serving and helping others and doing so out of love.

> And now, compelled by the Spirit, I am going to Jerusalem, not knowing what will happen to me there. (Acts 20:22 NIV)

Who do you like to work with?

Who do you like to work with? Do you like to work with children, teenagers, young adults, parents, single people, newly married couples, elderly people, or some other audience? What audience? What type of person?

I love to work with leaders who want to grow and be successful. That matches up with my gift of leadership. Remember, there is only one you. God designed you for a special purpose, to be unique and different. Do not compare; rather, know yourself and gain clarity so you can design and align your life to be all God wants you to be. Don't try to be anyone else. Be you, who God designed you to be!

I didn't always have this level of clarity. I prayed about and asked these questions of myself until the answers came. I wanted to make sure I was aligned and focused to be all God wanted me to be. Some of the questions took longer to answer than others. I share that with you to encourage you to stay the course. I don't want you to think this happens overnight. It's a process. If answers don't come to you right away, keep asking them and writing down the answers. Ask God for help. God places burdens in your heart to help others. Know that your burdens link to your purpose. You may find that as you go through various stages in life, your answers change, and that is okay. As we go through different stages of spiritual growth, God transforms us. As a result, you may have different answers at different stages of your life. If you need help, use this book in your small group so you can have the support of other believers and encourage one another.

What roles do you enjoy that link to those passions and burdens or problems?

For example, volunteer, employee, manager, director, leader, or assistant to a leader.

Be sure to write your answers on your profile under step 2. When completed, you will gain valuable insight to your sweet spot. This will enable you to align to God's divine design, make a difference in the lives of others, and glorify God.

Step 3: Experiences and Environment

SWEET SPOT

What experiences and environments have you worked or served in?

The goal here is threefold—gain insight, learn from, and identify what you enjoy the most and where you can have the greatest impact based upon your experiences and environments. Doing so helps you make good choices to get into your sweet spot. This is where you are going to have the maximum impact to bless others, maximum contribution to the Kingdom of God to do the work of God, and maximum joy, including work/life satisfaction. It's all part of God's divine design for your life.

> Have you experienced so much in vain—if it really
> was in vain? (Galatians 3:4 NIV)

Experiences

- These can include extracurricular activities in the community, in sports or music, or at school. The key is to not waste these experiences.

Work

- Experiences in various roles, industries, and projects.

Education

- What degrees do you have? What courses or certifications have you completed?

Ministry

- At church, in the community, and in the workplace.

Values

- What are your top three values?

What environment or culture did you enjoy the most?

This is a question people seldom ask. When this is neglected, they often end up serving or working in a culture they don't enjoy. Pay attention to the environment, what you learned, and where you flourished in the past. You are not designed to survive;

instead, you are designed to thrive. Examples may include a team environment, a culture that is collaborative, purpose driven, structured, unstructured, high performing, growing, customer focused, entrepreneurial, or something else.

How can you learn about an environment or culture?

You can look at their values and talk to people who serve or work there. Values are often posted on websites. Values are important because they shape the behaviors of the people.

If you are a leader of an organization or of volunteers at church, it is important to communicate values, teach, and lead to align people to those values. Successful leaders do this consistently. I have seen so many professionals take new positions and not pay any attention to the culture or values, only to find that the environment is not matched with how God designed them. You have a choice to align to God's divine design and get into your sweet spot where you can have fun and flourish. Choose wisely!

What did you like about your experiences, and what do you want to build upon?

Keep in mind, your answers may change depending upon the stage of life. For example, someone just starting their career may choose to build upon experiences whereby they can connect with other people at the same stage of life. Our church used to have groups organized by age to match the stage of life one was at. We had a twenties group, thirties, forties, fifties, sixties, and retired. If you are retired, you may choose to build upon experiences that offer more people interaction. One woman worked in finance with numbers. That's what she enjoyed doing. When she retired, she said she wanted to work with people because she no longer had the people interaction she got at work. That was a great insight on her part to be open to how God was leading her and how she wanted to serve at that specific stage of her life.

My husband and I volunteered in several areas at church, such as serving communion, being a sounding board and mentor for the senior high pastor, leaders with a senior high retreat, and serving in the community. Individually, I designed and taught classes. While it was a privilege to serve communion and fun to spend time with the kids, my favorites were supporting the pastor and teaching. I like to work with leaders and to teach, mentor, and coach people to help them succeed. That's where God gifted me. You may not know the areas of service you enjoy most until you start serving. The key is to just start! You will learn as you go. Here are a few suggestions to get off to a strong start.

Pray and ask God to reveal to you the areas He wants you to build upon. Once you hear from God and align to His will and design to serve in that area—once you identify your sweet spot—you can say yes to opportunities that fall within the sweet spot and no to things that fall outside your sweet spot. That will free up energy, time, and resources to do what God designed you to do.

Step 4: Excellence and Energy

SWEET SPOT

What do you excel at?

God designed you to be the best, to excel at specific things. We call these abilities. Capabilities are abilities developed into skills and used to express one's potential.

We have all heard the quote "The enemy of best is good." There are many things a person can do; however, God designed you to be best and to focus on what you are best at!

In life, focusing on your sweet spot, God's divine design to serve others and honor God, enables you to make the greatest contribution to the Kingdom of God and bless others.

Paul wrote that all believers should be "careful to devote themselves to doing what is good.

This is a trustworthy saying. And I want you to stress these things, so that those who have trusted in God may be careful to devote themselves to doing what is good. These things are excellent and profitable for everyone" (Titus 3:8 NIV).

The problem is that many people don't know what they do best or are not focused on it. When this happens, people try to do everything and then end up exhausted and stop serving. How can you avoid exhaustion that leads to burnout? Focus on what you excel at and do it better than anyone else for the glory of God.

I remember when our small group leader at church asked me to fill in for her while she was on vacation. I walked through the principles in this book, and one woman was relieved to know she no longer had to try to do it all. She was spreading herself so thin pursuing multiple opportunities. They were all good opportunities; however, pursuing all the good things left her feeling exhausted.

After helping her understand and align to God's divine design and get into her sweet spot, she stopped doing five things and chose to do one that helped her maximize her contribution to bless others and honor God. You should have seen the expression on her face. She was so excited that she had ignited her God-given potential!

I use my sweet spot and profile as a filter for what I say yes to. I say yes to serving at church in areas that require leadership, teaching, and speaking; that's what I love to do. Even though there are a lot of other opportunities to serve, I say no to the majority of those because someone else in the church body can do it better with their God-given design. There are exceptions, like if my pastor needs help in another area. Most of my serving is done in my sweet spot so I can have the maximum impact for God.

We can be good at many things; however, we were designed to be excellent at few! Once you identify the abilities you are best at, then you can develop the ability to create a capability. Excellence, energy, and passion go together. This will help you prioritize your time to avoid exhaustion and give you energy to maximize your kingdom impact.

> For we are His workmanship, created in Christ Jesus for good works, which God prepared beforehand that we should walk in them. (Ephesians 2:10 NKJV)

What is the biblical definition of ability?

Ability can be defined as the capacity to do something. I think of it as using everything God gives us to do with excellence to honor God. That means our resources, materials (mental and spiritual), and gifts. Exodus 35:30–33 describes how God filled Bezalel with His power and the ability to work in wood and engage in all kinds of artistic work.

The word *ability* refers to a person's potential to do/achieve something when there's a high chance that they will do it successfully. *Capability* is the aptitude or skill to do it.

Ability	Capability
Jim understands what it takes to be a good leader and has potential to be a good leader.	Mary developed her leadership ability into a skill and demonstrated great leadership to lead her team of volunteers to serve meals for one hundred people on Saturday.

The Holy Spirit gives us grace and supernatural power to do certain things with excellence.

It is not in our own power but rather via grace and the power of the Holy Spirit under the direction of the Holy Spirit to bless others and advance God's kingdom.

Develop your abilities into capabilities by learning, growing, and using them to serve others and honor God. Complete your profile at the back of the book in milestone five.

The Bible says training and development are important to being a good servant. All scripture is God breathed and is useful for training in righteousness, so that the servant of God may be thoroughly equipped for every good work (1 Timothy 4:6–10). God wants us to develop our abilities, our spiritual gifts, and our talents.

In Daniel 1:17, God gave Daniel great ability. Daniel honored God by being a good steward of what God gave him. God gave these four young men—Daniel, Hananiah, Mishael, and Azariah—an unusual aptitude for understanding every aspect of literature and wisdom, and God gave Daniel the special ability to understand and interpret the meanings of all kinds of visions and dreams.

Daniel soon proved himself more capable than all the other administrators and high officers. Because of Daniel's great ability, the king made plans to place him over the entire empire.

> We have different gifts, according to the grace
> given to each of us. (Romans 12:6a NIV)

Where do our abilities come from? From our great God! What are they for? To bless others and please God. God gives us everything we need to do His will. When we focus on what we do best, it pleases God and adds value to people.

> Equip you with everything good for doing his will,
> and may he work in us what is pleasing to him,
> through Jesus Christ, to whom be glory for ever
> and ever. Amen. (Hebrews 13:21 NIV)

We have all seen people who are not enthusiastic about their jobs. What would happen if you aligned your work, or anything else you do, to God's divine design for your life? Your work/life satisfaction would soar. You would be able to add value to more people's lives!

Think about your children who may be in college or starting a career. What if they chose to work in an area where they can be their best and excel? They would have a lot of success and be able to make a difference in the lives of others, all for the glory of God.

Age and stage of life don't matter. Even someone retired can choose to do what they do best to serve at church or in the community.

What are you excellent or best at? Write down the answer under step 4 on your profile.

What energizes you?

There are certain things that give you energy; doing them doesn't seem like work. Look back at your spiritual gifts, specifically your motivational gifts. Your motivational gifts are what drive you. It's how you approach things. This will provide insight into your perspective on life, work, and everything you do.

Helping people energizes me. I have always been highly driven. Ever since I was young, I recognized that I needed to find a way to channel all my energy in a positive way. When I learned about motivational gifts, I discovered that all three of my gifts were motivational gifts. This is one reason I have so much drive. The other reason is all because of my relationship with God. It's how God designed me and led me to discover and develop my sweet spot, the area I can have the greatest impact for God.

I remember talking with an executive who volunteered to work with disabled adults to make cabinets. It was very meaningful to him because he had a son who was disabled. That's a great example of how he used a painful experience to serve and help others. He would get so excited when he would talk about it. He was energized by doing something purposeful.

I remember hearing a teenager say during winter break, "I am lazy." It broke my heart. She was not lazy; she just hadn't figured out what motivated her and how to motivate herself. Frequently, students who are in sports or music are in highly structured programs at school and don't have any downtime. When they finally do have unstructured downtime, they don't feel motivated. I believe you need to know yourself to grow yourself. When you grow in your sweet spot, you will be energized and motivated. Don't rely on others to motivate you.

How do we know ourselves? By understanding what God says about who we are and how He designed us. By seeking and knowing God more, we seek and know ourselves more. By partnering with God to fulfill His vision and mission, recognizing we are part of His epic story. Lastly, by believing in faith that God knows best, trusting Him, receiving His direction, and taking action to understand and do what God wants you to do.

Write your answer to the question "What energizes you?" under step 4 on your profile. Once you start to discover and align to your God-given design, you will find energy and motivation. You will come alive and ignite your God-given potential!

Step 5: Temperament

SWEET SPOT

What is temperament? It is your nature, how you are wired and how it affects your behavior. Temperament is not our entire personality; however, it does affect our personality.

It's important to not put yourself or other people in a box. We are complex in our design, and when we are in a relationship with God, studying God's Word, and seeking to know God more, we are continually being transformed. Therefore, use this section to gain insight into your temperament and how it may influence your personality.

As we discussed earlier, be sensitive to others and flexible when their temperament is different from yours. Tailor your approach to effectively communicate with, build up, and encourage others. Acting out of love and compassion with yourself and others aligns with how God wants you to behave.

> And there are diversities of activities, but it is the same
> God who works all in all. (1 Corinthians 12:6 NKJV)

As you review this list, circle the traits on your profile under step 5 that match your temperament. Keep in mind, your traits are how God designed you. By embracing your uniqueness, using what God gave you to serve others and honor God, you ignite your potential and align to God's divine design.

- introvert or extrovert

    > This is one of the most misunderstood traits. Some people think that an introvert doesn't like people, but that is not what this means. Introverts get their energy alone. Extroverts get their energy with people. It's about where you get your energy.

- self-expressive or self-controlled
- prefer routine or variety
- disciplined or undisciplined
- collaborative or competitive
- planner or spontaneous
- structure or no structure
- high drive or low drive
- risk taker or prefer less risk
- slow pace or fast pace
- thinker or feeler

Do you lead with a thoughtful approach, reflect, and think before you speak, or do you lead with your feelings? If you are a feeler, you may check the feelings of those you are interacting with and relate to them via feeling first.

Keep in mind, there is no right or wrong. Embrace who God designed you to be. Once again, these will give you clues and valuable insight into God's divine design. In that context, think about your family. Think about your spouse, children, parents, or siblings. What is each person's temperament? How about your friends? How about at work? What is the temperament of your colleagues, your boss, or your subordinates?

Knowing what you know now, how can you change your approach to have flexibility and fit, embracing God's divine design in relationships with others? In other words, if a family member is an introvert and you are an extrovert, how can you honor their need to recharge by being alone instead of with people? If you like structure and work for a boss who doesn't like structure, how can you tailor your approach and communication to have a healthy relationship and honor who God designed your boss to be? Valuing God's divine design in yourself and in others is essential to building healthy relationships and honoring God.

Complete step 5 on your profile before moving to step 6.

Step 6: Set Goals to Serve and Grow!

SWEET SPOT

Pray and ask God for help and to direct your steps.

Why are goals important?

- Goals direct and focus us. They help us become good stewards of what God has given us. They help us run our race with endurance. The enemy wants to distract you. Don't fall into that trap. Focus on what God wants you to focus on, which is serving, helping others, and glorifying God.

- Goals help us build upon our strengths and gifts.
- Goals help us steward what God gives us to glorify God and help others.
- Goals stretch us and motivate us. When someone struggles with motivation, I ask them, "What goals are you working on right now?" The answer is usually "I don't have goals." No wonder you are not motivated. Set goals!
- They help us live life to the fullest. I don't want to live a life of regret, saying, "I wish I would have or could have." Instead, I want to say, "I am thankful I glorified God with what He gave me. I am thankful I used my gifts, talents, and abilities to help others and honor God to the best of my ability."
- Goals increase our likelihood of success. The probability of completing any goal increases by 50 percent if you plan out how you will accomplish your goal. Write your goals down on your profile.

Set goals to serve.

We can all have good intentions, but my experience is that faith requires action. We honor God by letting His priorities become our priorities. One priority God has for all of us is to serve others. Instead of trying to fit God into your schedule, start by making a commitment to serve and pray for what God wants you to do in this season. We make time when we commit to God's agenda first. Because our lives are devoted to God, His agenda takes priority. Lastly, instead of thinking of serving as an event or a task, I have learned to view serving as a lifestyle. Every one of us can serve others daily by praying and asking the Holy Spirit to use us to bless people God puts in our path to glorify God. I keep a prayer list on my phone, so I remember who to pray for. Currently,

I have sixteen women whom I pray for daily and a goal to start my day praying for each person. If I don't set a goal to pray for them every morning, the day can get so busy that I forget to pray. Goals help us stay focused on what matters most. It also helps me to be consistent, praying for others daily. Personally, I want to bless others and glorify God daily out of love for God. Setting goals helps us steward what God gives us and to be intentional about serving.

When you set goals, make sure they are SMART goals.

Specific, measurable, attainable, relevant, and trackable (SMART) goals are the key to success. The more specific you are, the more likely you are to succeed. The goal should be attainable but also stretch you to reach your full potential. Goals should be relevant to you, your generation, and what God is asking you to do. Trackable simply means a goal should have a timeframe (e.g., within thirty days or by a certain date). That way, you can measure your progress in achieving the goal.

The profile in the back of the book contains an example of thirty-, sixty-, and ninety-day SMART goals.

Write down your thirty-, sixty-, and ninety-day goals under step 6.

Set goals to grow. This is essential to ignite your potential.

What's the difference between an athlete who wins the race and one who finishes in third place? A desire and discipline to grow. The difference between world-class athletes and average ones is that little extra, the desire to grow and complete disciplined training to get better and be their best. I love to watch the top five marathon runners compete to win. I remember going with my husband to cheer on the marathoners at the Twin Cities marathon. As the runners passed us, I said, "He is going to win. I could see it on his face. He had winning on his mind. He trained with discipline, and he was running with confidence. You can tell when someone has trained with discipline and has the hunger to do their best." Sure enough, he won the race, but not by more than a couple minutes. Training gives you a competitive advantage. Winners commit to setting growth goals. God designed you to reign in life, to live in victory. You were born to be a winner, not a loser. Set goals to grow, to develop your spiritual gifts and all God has given you to bless others. The more you grow, the more you will have to give. Remember, when God needs something done, He will look to the Christian who has developed their spiritual gifts and has a heart to serve others in alignment with His will. Write down your thirty-, sixty-, and ninety-day growth goals under step 6 on your profile before you move to step 7.

Step 7: Pray for Purpose

SWEET SPOT

Prayer changes everything. God's power is released when we ask for help. God wants you to run into His arms and ask for help. Nobody can reveal your purpose to you better than God who created you. You will find an example of a prayer in step 7 on your profile.

Purpose

Gain insight into your individual purpose by answering these questions and writing your answers on your profile.

- What dream(s) has God placed in your heart?
- What is the number one thing God wants to accomplish through you to influence others for Christ?
- What needs has He placed before you?
- How does that advance God's kingdom?
- What does God want you to do in your lifetime?
- What do you want to say to the next generation?

One of the things I found very confusing is that there are multiple terms used to describe the same thing in books, sermons, and among leaders, yet none are defined. As God continued to transform my heart's desire to know Him more, I was trying to figure out what God was calling me to do. I reached out to my pastor and asked him for a list of books he recommended on God's purpose and calling. When his assistant sent me the list, I found that I had already read half of them, yet I was still so confused by what the terms *purpose*, *calling*, and *destiny* meant. I found that each book and each pastor used a different definition. When I asked pastors about it, I received different answers. After five more years of studying, praying, and seeking, finally I gained more clarity. My intent is to save you the time and frustration of trying to figure this out all by yourself.

The Bible uses both *purpose* and *calling*. Very simply, your individual purpose is the same as your calling or destiny. I am going to share definitions of these terms based upon what I have learned. While there are many purposes for a Christian, there is only one individual purpose. God designed you for a specific purpose that nobody else can fulfill.

How do we define your individual purpose, also known as your calling or destiny? Your individual purpose is your customized calling from God to do the work of God according to *His* purpose. Your destiny, as defined by Pastor Tony Evans, is your customized life calling, for which God has equipped and ordained you in order to bring Him the greatest glory and maximum expansion of His kingdom.

The Bible is full of people God called: Noah, Abraham, Moses, David, Mary, Joseph, and the apostle Paul. All were called to fulfill an individual purpose.

By reading the text and answering the questions on your profile under step 7, you will gain value insight into your individual purpose. The questions outlined here match your profile.

What dreams has God placed in your heart to bless others and honor Him? When we accept Jesus Christ as our Savior, repent of our sins, and invite Him to be the Lord of our life, God transforms us. He gives a new heart and places dreams inside of us. Some people stifle these dreams with fear, doubt, or excuses. Then they go to the grave full of dreams and potential that was never realized. What a tragedy to never fulfill the dreams and potential God placed inside of you. Don't let that tragedy happen to you. If you have doubts or lack clarity, keep praying about it and ask God for help to understand His plan and purpose for your life. God will help you gain clarity and overcome any obstacle, such as doubt. You are fully resourced, equipped to do whatever God places in your heart by trusting in God, depending on God, and seeking His guidance to realize these dreams, fulfilling His plan and purpose for your life.

Why is this important? Your individual purpose is connected to a dream God places in your heart. The dream is like a seed placed in your heart. He gives us line of sight from start to finish but not the details or the how to achieve it. Everything you need to fulfill your dreams is inside of you. A seed is complete. That means God has fully equipped you to fulfill the dreams He placed in your heart. The problem is that many people don't know those dreams are from God or how to develop them. All seeds start out in the dark; they need to be watered and need the right soil conditions to sprout up above the ground. To grow, one needs to know to become aware of the dream and to prepare the soil so the dream seed can sprout. To grow and to fulfill your dream, you need to seek God's plan and purpose and depend on God to fulfill His purpose and plan for your life. You will not be able to fulfill it on your own. You need other believers and God's guidance. God is the God of the how and when. He knows exactly how to lead you and help you fulfill the dream, plan, and purpose. He put the dream inside of you!

When we align to God's divine design, we participate in His divine nature. When we lay ahold of His divine promises, study His

Word, and seek to trust, know, and obey God, we water and prepare the soil. This helps the seed to grow.

Jesus said in the parable of a seed that is starts off small and grows large:

He told them another parable: "The kingdom of heaven is like a mustard seed, which a man took and planted in his field. Though it is the smallest of all seeds, yet when it grows, it is the largest of garden plants and becomes a tree, so that the birds come and perch in its branches." (Matthew 13:31–32 NIV)

When we pray for God to transform the desires of our hearts and we seek to know Him better and do His will, the dreams come alive. It's never too late to rekindle those dreams.

> The second problem is that people often extinguish their dreams. Some go so far as to say they will never achieve their dreams. They don't always realize that when they do, they are extinguishing God in themselves. Don't do that! You will never realize your full God-given potential by extinguishing the dream God gave you. It's your job to tend to your flame and to pursue the dream God placed in your heart.

I love what Pastor Wayne Cordeiro, author of the book *Dream Releasers*, says:

> Everybody has ... A dream. His dream placed intentionally inside you is like a seed. Within that seed's protective shell is contained all the latent possibilities of producing an expansive orchard or a great forest. It holds the ability to feed a city. It can yield warmth in winter or it can produce houses for new families. *But unless that potential is recognized and released,* it remains richly unproductive,

helplessly filled with hope and powerfully impotent.
But once discovered, it becomes a honing device,
an invisible guide that navigates us through the
precarious passages of life. (p. 27)

Make a list of your dreams.

One woman in my small group was so excited when I walked through this. She told me, "In the past, I didn't have time to dream." She had been through a divorce and was a single parent. Every day, she was trying to survive. When I led a small group study on spiritual gifts and purpose, she said, "For the first time, I started to dream. When you were talking, I was writing as fast as I could. All the dreams started to flow." She had renewed and restored hope and enthusiasm for what God was going to do in her life. When I talked to her last weekend, it was evident she was fulfilling the dream God placed in her heart and was serving in her sweet spot!

Pray and ask God to reveal to you the dream He gave you that aligns with what He wants you to do, along with when and where He gave it to you.

I remember thirty years ago when God placed a dream in my heart. We were at church, sitting about five chairs to the left of the aisle. At the time, I did not know anything about this process. As I prepared the soil, watered the seed, and spent the next thirty years seeking to know God better, love God more, and make Him a priority in my life, God gave me clarity on how I could fulfill that dream. As I look back, I can see how He shifted me into alignment and placed people in my path to work toward fulfilling that dream. Before a dream sprouts, one needs to develop the root by studying God's Word, developing their relationship with God, surrendering, and obeying God. The dream reveals who God wants you to become and is linked to God's overall purpose for your life, serving others and advancing God's kingdom. Who God wants us to become is part of our individual purpose.

Why am I sharing this with you? I don't want you to miss the dream God places in your heart. Even if it is beneath the soil, get started right now in aligning to God's divine design for your life. It is a process, and we don't determine the timing; God does. When we are faithful with the little things, and when God has developed our character to trust us with more, then He gives us more and does more through us. God decides the best time to call you. God knows when you are ready, so wait patiently upon the Lord. Do not try to take control of or rush the process. Do the work and be patient. Wait on God's timing. God's timing is always perfect.

Once you discover the dream God placed inside of you to contribute to His kingdom, pursue it with your whole heart. Join a church and a small group because you will need other believers to fulfill that dream. You won't be able to fulfill it on your own.

Some people receive their purpose or calling at an early age; others receive it later. In other words, for some, it is gradual and later in life. *Ask yourself, "What is the number one thing I believe God wants to accomplish through me to influence others for Christ?"*

Keep in mind that if you don't have the answer to this question right away, keep asking and praying about it! Ask God to reveal it to you. I asked, prayed, and journaled about some of these questions for years before I gained full clarity. Some will come right away, and others may take time. Don't give up! Answering these questions leads to your individual calling, purpose, and God's plan for your life, and that is worth pursuing!

For me, God's call on my life has been gradual. When I became a Christian, I knew that I was designed for God and to live to glorify God and help others, but my more specific individual purpose came later in life. God reveals our individual purpose and calling as we surrender, trust, obey, and seek to know Him more daily and to glorify Him. God reveals Himself more as we seek Him, study, and meditate on His Word. We have an active role of seeking God, studying, meditating on His Word, trusting Him to lead us, and obeying God, and we have a passive role of receiving His love. Our job is also to align and position our hearts to God's heart to do what God designed us and wants us to do. As we obey Him and help the people He puts in front of us, He reveals more to us. God works out our purpose and plan for His purposes. When we align and partner with God, we experience great joy and maximum impact for His kingdom.

For me, clarity came from seeking to know God more, studying His Word, and praying to God. Doing so helps me hear His voice as He reveals Himself more and more. God places the needs of others in our path, which gives us an opportunity to serve others.

What needs has God placed in front of you? This can be in the workplace or your community, neighborhood, or family. The call is linked to other people's needs—needs God puts in front of us to serve others out of the love of Christ. How we respond to those needs is important. Will we serve others and help them satisfy those needs? God reveals Himself to us as we serve others. The more we help others and honor God by helping others, the more responsibility we receive. In other words, serving others with little things matures us to take on greater responsibility. *How does it advance God's kingdom? How have you responded?* Our response to serve others and honor God is an act of faith and obedience.

The Bible teaches us that as we are faithful with little things, God can trust us with more.

> And if you have not been trustworthy with someone else's property, who will give you property of your own? (Luke 16:12 NIV)

Why is that so important? Because the Holy Spirit reveals insight and understanding unavailable through any other means. This includes revelation of God's plans and purposes as well as helpful knowledge of the keys to solving seemingly unsolvable challenges.

> But God has revealed them to us through His Spirit. For the Spirit searches all things, yes, the deep things of God. For what man knows the things of a man except the spirit of the man which is in him? Even so no one knows the things of God except the Spirit of God. Now we have received, not the spirit of the world, but the Spirit who is from God, that we might know the things that have been freely given to us by God. (1 Corinthians 2:10–12 NKJV)

What is the number one thing you believe God wants to accomplish through you to influence others for Christ? It may not be convenient or even make sense. I've learned the key is to do it anyway. God knows what you need and knows what others need before we know what we need. Doing what God directs us to is an act of trusting and obeying God out of love. Who do you trust more, yourself or God? God wants us to trust Him more.

For the last ten years, people have asked me about spiritual gifts, or God has put me in conversations with people about spiritual gifts and purpose. I did some work with the next generation and listened to them say that their entire generation lacked purpose. They said they didn't know God had a plan and purpose for their life. When I learned that so many people didn't know their purpose or what the Bible said about spiritual gifts, my heart ached. I prayed and asked how I could help them. God gave me a burden to help people discover their spiritual gifts, find their purposes, and align to God's divine design for their lives. These needs and this burden are all part of God's plan. God has a plan for you too! After praying, I answered God's call to teach a course on spiritual gifts, and a couple years later, God asked me to write this book. When we obey with the little things, God gives us more.

I was really excited at first. Then, as I got started, I met a lot of opposition. Writing this book was hard. You see, I didn't know exactly how all this was going to come together, but I remembered what one of our pastors said: "God is the God of how and when." I learned that we don't need to know the how and when to do what God asks us to do. The key is to trust God and just start. You see, I felt unqualified. God reminded me, "I don't call the equipped; I equip the called." That gave me assurance that He would equip me. That's where faith comes in to believe in God for the unseen and trust Him to perform His Word in me and through me. As I trusted God, He revealed to me everything He did to prepare me for the past forty years. After all, He led me to discover and develop my spiritual gifts and help others do the same for nearly thirty years before He called me to write this book. He reminded me of the dream He placed in my heart over thirty years ago. He gave me clarity of vision with a picture of what He wanted me to do. Keep in mind that vision and clarity came after thirty years of serving, studying, and seeking to know God better and do what He guided me to do. This was followed by five years of testing, opposition, multiple big leaps of faith, and patience as I waited for God to reveal the right time when I was ready to take the next step and write this book. I learned the key to fulfilling God's plans, purpose, and dreams is to take big leaps of faith and trust God to do His work through you. Dreams don't come true by talking about them. We need action for dreams to be realized. We become more by taking big leaps of faith toward trusting and depending on God. Why big leaps of faith? Because baby steps won't get you there. God has a plan and purpose for your life too!

It's a big plan and purpose to make a difference in the lives of others and to advance His kingdom. Big dreams require big leaps of faith. I want to encourage you to trust God, depend on Him, and take steps of faith to fulfill His plan. Expect opposition, but also know that God is a breakthrough God, and when you partner with God, He will break through all opposition and hindrance to ensure His plan prevails.

If you don't know the answers to these questions, pray to the Holy Spirit and ask Him to reveal to you what God is calling you to do in this lifetime. Be sure to write down the answers on your profile.

Prayer:

"Lord, I dedicate my life to You and want to honor You with everything I say, think, and do. Thank You for your divine design. Thank You for blessing me with a relationship with You for eternity. Holy Spirit, reveal to me what You are calling me to do in this lifetime. What problems do You want me to help people overcome. What needs have You placed in front of me that You want me to help people overcome? Reveal to me the needs of those You want me to serve today and guide me to respond to them in a loving way. I want to be faithful in serving You daily. I know serving daily is an act of worship to honor You. I say, 'Yes, God,' to serve the needs of those You put in my path today. In Jesus's name, I pray. Amen."

Secondly, study what the Bible says about your purpose.

Here are a few verses to get you started. The Bible uses the word *calling* in addition to the word *purpose*. While we have multiple purposes as Christians, we have one individual purpose, calling, or destiny. It's amazing how our God has a personal calling for each one of us.

> For you created my inmost being; you knit me together in my mother's womb. I praise you because I am fearfully and wonderfully made; your works are wonderful, I know that full well. My frame was

> not hidden from you when I was made in the secret place, when I was woven together in the depths of the earth. Your eyes saw my unformed body; all the days ordained for me were written in your book before one of them came to be. (Psalm 139:13–16 NIV)

> Before I formed you in the womb I knew you, before you were born I set you apart; I appointed you as a prophet to the nations. (Jeremiah 1:5 NIV)

It's a privilege to be called. When I was challenged to fulfill the call to write this book, God revealed to me that it is a privilege to be called. I thanked God from that day forward for asking me to write this book. God changed my attitude and turned my "have to" into "get to." Today, I get to spend time with God, and today, I get to depend on Him and obey His call to write. Here is a favorite verse to encourage you:

> And I thank Christ Jesus our Lord who has enabled me, because He counted me faithful, putting me into the ministry. (1 Timothy 1:12 NKJV)

God always equips and empowers us to do what He calls us to do. God places the needs of people in front of us and links satisfying those needs to advance His purpose and plan. Being kind and blessing others out of love, honors God.

> The one who calls you is faithful, and he will do it. (1 Thessalonians 5:24 NIV)

What do you want to say to the next generation? The answer to this question stems from the needs God places in your heart to serve the next generation.

If you are not aware of others' needs, maybe it is because you are focused on yourself instead of others. Ask God to reveal to you the needs of others.

Hearing the voice of God comes from spending time with God and spending time studying God's Word by reading the Bible. That is the primary way God speaks to us—through His living Word. Nothing replaces the need to know and understand God's Word.

The more we fill ourselves up with God's Word, read the Bible, pray, ask to be used by God to serve others, and honor God, the more He reveals Himself to us. If you struggle with clarity, posture your heart to God's heart and seek to know God better, to love God more, and to love and serve God's people.

Know that God can speak to you through a prompting, such as to help someone out of love, a word, a need He places in front of you, a picture, a correction to repent from a sin and to obey, a sense of knowing, a peace within, and, of course, through His Word.

What would I say to the next generation? Everything in this book. In summary, ignite your potential and align to God's divine design! Discover your spiritual gifts, find your purpose, and get into your sweet spot to fulfill God's amazing plan for your life.

Lastly, you will be rewarded in heaven for doing the work of God on earth. Personally, I want to do God's work out of love for God, not for a prize. At the same time, God wants us to know He will reward us. God wants to bless us with the joy of spending eternity with Him and living according to His divine design.

> I press toward the goal for the prize of the upward
> call of God in Christ Jesus. (Philippians 3:14 NKJV)

From all you've learned, write out your individual purpose statement on your profile, what God designed you to contribute to serve the needs of others and His kingdom.

In the upper room, when Jesus was concluding his last day before the cross, he washed his disciples' feet and said,

> "Now that you know these things, you will be blessed if you do them." (John 13:17 NIV)

Once you know what God wants you to do, the blessing comes when you commit to trusting God and doing it with your whole heart.

That is what happened to me. In October 2020, as I was doing my strategic plan for 2021, I prayed for God to give me a word to plan my year around. As I mentioned earlier, I have done this for nearly thirty years. God always gives me a word in October. The word he gave me was WRITE. This was the first time the word was in all caps! As the new year started, I was so excited because I prayed, and God gave me clarity on writing this book. During a flight, I outlined all the chapters. Then, every day, I wrote.

Then came the opposition. All the chapters became a blur, and then I wondered if God really wanted me to write this book. I did a lot of writing in 2021; however, I felt like I was at a standstill. In October 2021, I prayed for a word for my 2022 strategic plan. God gave me the word *worship*. He knew I needed to shift my eyes to Him and seek His help, because in my heart, I wanted to do His will, but I didn't know how. I needed His help. This is exactly where God wants us to be. To rely and depend on Him to accomplish whatever He asks us to do. That doubt is the enemy trying to prevent us from doing the work of God. Once I realized that and began to worship God, He removed that doubt.

After a lot more work and still not getting clarity, in the first week of August, I committed to writing the first draft of the book by the end of September. I shared that with my husband and said, "No matter what, I am going to get this done." The very next day, everything came together. This was followed by more opposition. Dependence on God and reliance on His promises and Word removed all obstacles and hindrances.

I learned it all starts with commitment. Once you commit, start taking steps of faith, and ask God for help, He steps in. We are made strong in our weakness. As we step out in faith, God's Spirit and power fill us up and take us places we can't go on our own.

Step 8: Observe

SWEET SPOT

Write down observations. Identify three Christians who have observed you serving at church. Ask them, "What did you observe when you saw me serve?" Others often see potential in you that you don't see yourself. When you serve, God's family confirms your gifts in action.

Step 9: Transform

SWEET SPOT

A Christian life is a transformed life. I remember having lunch with a friend who said, "I am looking forward to seeing what God will do next in my life." I have thought about that comment for years. I learned to look forward in expectation of what God will do next in my life. Not only does He transform us, but He also transforms others through us as we serve.

- What did God do through you to transform the life of someone else?
- What fruit did God produce in the lives of others through your serving?
- What did God do in your heart as you served others and honored God?

How can you tell if your spiritual gift is confirmed in God's church? By the fruit. Your spiritual gifts, when used for the glory of God to bless others, will bear fruit. Seeing lives changed for the better by being a vessel for the Holy Spirit to work through is exhilarating. God wants to use you to positively impact the lives of others. God wants to use you to advance His kingdom, to magnify Christ from the altar of your life. You are needed both in and outside God's church. God designed you with a purpose and a plan to bless others and to glorify Him wherever you go. Your neighborhood, friends, and family need you. Your workplace needs you. Start serving by helping others and glorifying God today!

Step 10: Pull It All Together

Find your individual purpose.

You were designed for significance: to serve, to grow, and to glorify God!

Answering the questions on your profile will provide clues to your individual purpose and help you gain clarity on your sweet spot.

Write out your individual purpose statement. From what you have learned, fill in the blanks under step 10 in your profile.

When _____(who) struggles with _____(problems), I help

them _____(do what), which gives God and me great joy.

You will have an opportunity to pull it all together and write your individual purpose statement on your profile in step 10.

Congratulations on your progress thus far. You are almost done. Simply fill in the blanks on your profile, pray, and seek God's guidance to gain clarity on our individual purpose. You may need to write it out three to five times, pray about it, and revise it until you are confident it is aligned to God's divine design and to advance God's kingdom.

Don't worry if you don't have all the answers. Clarity comes with action, so if you don't see it right away, keep working on it and praying. Remember, when you get into your sweet spot and align to God's divine design, you are posturing your heart to align with

God's heart to bless others, glorify God, and experience the following:

- maximum kingdom impact
- maximum work/life satisfaction and fulfillment
- maximum contribution/impact

Remember, you have potential! Align to God's divine design to ignite your potential!

Be sure to complete your profile and action plan on the next four pages to find your individual purpose. You have something to contribute. You were designed for significance and to serve.

Discovery and Discussion Questions: Align to God's Divine Design and Ignite Your Potential!

My Profile
Name_____Date_____
Your Unique Design—Your Sweet Spot

❶	**S—Spiritual Gift(s)** **Top 1–3 Spiritual Gifts**	
❷	**W—What Do You Love to Do?** **Passion**	What do you love to do? What makes you happy? What makes you cry? Why? What burdens has God placed in your heart to help people? What causes are you passionate about? Who do you like to work with? What roles have you enjoyed the most?
❸	**E—Experiences and Environment** **Work** **Education** **Ministry** **Environment**	Experiences (positive and painful; include your testimony) Work Education Ministry What environment or culture did you enjoy the most? What are your top five values?

④	E—Excellence and Energy	What are you excellent or best at? What energizes you?
⑤	T—Temperament (a.k.a. Personality) **Circle the one that best describes you.**	• introvert or extrovert • self-expressive or self-controlled • prefer routine or variety • disciplined or undisciplined • collaborative or competitive • planner or spontaneous • structure or no structure • high drive or low drive • risk taker or prefer less risk • slow pace or fast pace • thinker or feeler

6 SPOT
Set Goals to Serve and Grow

My Ninety-Day Action Plan
to Serve and Grow

Name: _____ **Date:**_____

Prayer:

"Father, thank You for the privilege of being able to serve Your people and honor You with all You have given me. Lord, reveal to me the needs of those You put in my path who You want me to help. Transform my heart's desires to have compassion, to care for and help those You put in my path. Direct my steps to contribute and volunteer at church, in the community, and in the workplace. Show me what You are doing in the world and what You want my contribution to be in this season. I want to know You better, love You more, and honor You with my life. In Jesus's name, I pray. Amen."

Set Goals to Serve		
Thirty Days	**Sixty Days**	**Ninety Days**
Today I will go to our church website, look at the service opportunities that match my gifts, and sign up to serve.	I'll pray and ask the Holy Spirit to use me to glorify God daily. I'll listen to His prompting and make myself available to serve others.	I am going to develop my gift of hospitality by hosting a meal for our friends at my house every ninety days.

Set Goals to Grow Your Spiritual Gifts		
Thirty Days	**Sixty Days**	**Ninety Days**
I will have a friend take the spiritual gift assessment so we can share our gifts and support each other this month.	I am going to read a book on leadership to develop my leadership gift.	I will lead a small group with this book to bless others.

❼	SPOT **Pray for Purpose**	"Heavenly Father, thank You for designing me for a purpose and plan to bless others and honor You. Lord, reveal to me my individual purpose, the desires You placed in my heart to bless others, glorify You, and advance Your kingdom. Help me to gain clarity as I answer these questions to align with Your divine design, purpose, and plan for my life. In Jesus's name, I pray. Amen."
	SPOT **Purpose** **Gain insight into** **your individual purpose.**	What dream(s) has God placed in your heart? What is the number one thing God wants to accomplish through you to influence others for Christ? What needs has He placed before you? How does that advance God's kingdom? What does God want you to do in your lifetime? What do you want to say to the next generation?

⑧	SPOT **Observe**	Write down observations. Identify three Christians who have observed you serving and ask for their observations. God reveals our purpose as we serve. Other believers may see things you may not see.
⑨	SPOT **Transformation** **Changed Lives, Fruit**	What did God do through you to transform the life of someone else? What fruit did God produce in the lives of others through your serving? What did God do in your heart as you served others and honored God?
⑩	**Your Individual Purpose**	Write out your individual purpose statement. When _____(who) struggle with _____ (problems), I help them _____(do what), which gives God and me great joy.

Step 10: Pull It All Together

Align to God's divine design and ignite your potential!
What does that look like? What areas of your life do you need to shift into alignment to serve others and glorify God?

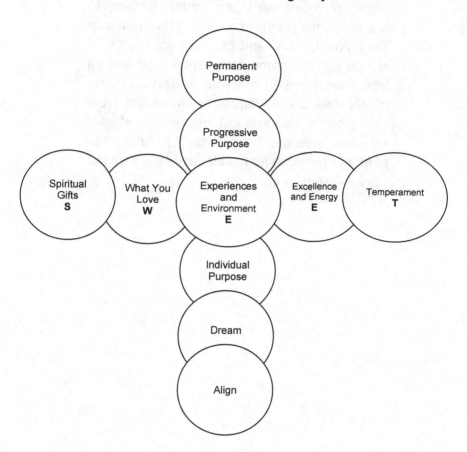

As you gain clarity on who you are in Christ, who God is, and His design for you, it will become easier to align to His divine design. The more you know God and love God, the easier it is to trust God and be all God designed you to be. Remember, the Holy Spirit will ignite your potential and guide you on your journey. This will enable you to steward your life to maximize your contribution to His kingdom.

Prayer:

"Holy Spirit, thank You for Your direction, purpose, and plan for my life. Reveal to me what You want me to say, think, and do to rearrange my priorities to be in alignment with Your Word, plan, and purpose for my life. I surrender and commit my whole self and all You have blessed me with to serve others, glorify You, and advance Your kingdom. Help me to honor You and get into my sweet spot so I can have maximum impact to fulfill Your plan and purpose for my life. In Jesus's name, I pray. Amen."

Discovery and Application Questions: Align to God's Divine Design and Ignite Your Potential

1. What did I learn?

2. What does the Holy Spirit want me to do today?

3. What can I apply or do to align to God's divine design?

Complete your profile and add your action items to your calendar, retake your assessment in milestone one ninety days from your initial date to review your progress, and update your serve and development plan for growth which is located in your profile. This plan can be updated with new goals every 90 days.

Don't extinguish your potential! Take action to ignite your potential and be all God designed you to be. As a leader in your church, what can you do to ignite the potential in your church to become all God designed your church to be?

Susan A. Lund

Thank you for joining me on this journey. In closing, I pray blessings over you. "May God continue to guide you in your journey to fulfill His plans and purpose for your life. May you discover and develop your spiritual gifts. May you get into your sweet spot, find your purpose, and align to God's amazing design for your life. I pray that you experience the joy that comes with serving others and glorifying God. May you say, 'Yes, God,' to whatever He wants to do in you and through you. May Christ be magnified from the altar of your life. Remember, you have potential! Align to God's divine design and ignite your potential! In Jesus's name, I pray. Amen."

I'll leave you with one of my favorite verses:

> For I know the thoughts that I think toward you, says the LORD, thoughts of peace and not of evil, to give you a future and a hope. (Jeremiah 29:11 NKJV)

God bless you!

Susan

To engage Susan to speak, train, consult, or coach, call 1-800-281-6084. We would love to help you, your team, or your church discover your spiritual gifts, find your purpose, and align to God's divine design to be all God designed you to be!

Appendix

Strategies for Churches to Use This Book

Incorporate the following into your growth strategy as a church. Why? To grow yourself, your family, and God's church. Ignite your potential, discover your spiritual gifts, find your purpose, align to God's divine design, and be all God designed you to be!

Recruit

- Utilize this tool to recruit staff. Take the spiritual gift assessment and discover God's purpose and vision for your life/career. Match with what is required for the position.

New Members

- Use the book in an orientation class for new members. Discover your spiritual gifts, find your purpose, and align to God's divine design. People depart with an action plan to serve, grow, and be all God designed them to be (a great differentiator to help your church with recruiting new members and retaining members).
- Use in outreach. Invite a friend to a small-group Bible study with this book to experience the joy of a growing relationship with our great God. God designed us to bless others with His blessings.

New or Existing Attendees

- Integrate this book in your "next steps" program for people to discover their spiritual gifts, find their purpose, and align to God's divine design. This gives people an opportunity to get to know your church, build relationships, and get involved by using the profile and action plans to serve in their sweet spot.
- People enjoy serving when utilizing their spiritual gifts. People stay at a church when they are involved, belong, and are becoming all God designed them to be.
- Complement your training and retention strategy by using this book in small groups.

Train—Equip

Grow Yourself, Grow Your Family, Grow God's Family

- Connect your family to God's family. We all know family members who could benefit from going to church, growing spiritually, and having a personal relationship with God. Of all the people we want to see experience the love of Christ, it's our family. Give this book to your family to connect to God's family. Learn and affirm one another's spiritual gifts.
- Sponsor a family; read this book together and discuss it.
- Use this book to complement your training strategy with a small-group Bible study.

Expand

New Church Plants or Churches You Want to Grow

1. Offer to outreach viewing groups or any of the above. They need a common foundation. A small-group study or course with this book is a great way viewing groups or new churches can grow together and be a light for Christ.

2. Share testimonials in small groups or at the beginning of a service of someone who discovered their gift and is now serving, using their gifts.

Discovery and Discussion Questions

-   What strategies are best for our church?
-   What strategies can help us have the greatest impact in our community?
-   Where can we apply these strategies to advance the Kingdom of God?

To engage Susan to speak, train, consult, or coach, call 1-800-281-6084. We would love to help you, your team, or your church discover your spiritual gifts, find your purpose, and align to God's divine design to be all God designed you to be! For more information, go to www.igniteyourpotential.org which is coming soon.

Roadblocks to Igniting Your Potential

1. *Priorities*

   Putting anything above God. If I were to ask you, "What are the three most important relationships in your life? List them in order," if God is not number one, that means your priorities do not honor God. This will prevent you from being all God designed you to be. Instead, always keep God as number one!

2. *Fear*

   Fear of any type, such as what people will think. The enemy uses fear to try to stop people from doing the work of God. You may feel fear, but you don't have to choose to be afraid. Being afraid is a choice. You can choose to trust God and walk in faith instead of fear. Don't let fear become a roadblock. The Bible says, "When I am afraid, I put my trust in you" (Psalm 56:3 NIV). Instead, pray, "Lord, I choose to put my trust in You. I choose faith over fear. In Jesus's name, I pray. Amen."

3. *Pride*

   Self-reliance, self-focused, and thinking your way is the only way, the right way. Pride is one of the enemy's most destructive tools. It's shifting our focus from God to ourselves. God wants us to be humble, which means not to think less of ourselves but to think of ourselves less. God wants us to shift our focus to Him instead of ourselves, to rely on God. To rely on God, we acknowledge His ways are higher than our ways, we need God in our life, and we are created to glorify God, to rely on God, and to serve others. Shift your focus to God. Instead, pray, "Lord, reveal to me any prideful thoughts or ways so I can repent, glorify You, depend on You, serve others, and be all You designed me to be."

4. ***Complacency***
    Complacency is staying in our comfort zone, believing a lie that it's better to play it safe than change and be transformed by God. As I stated in my previous book, *Ignite Your Selling Potential*, the comfort zone is a beautiful place, but nothing grows there. Playing it safe, not desiring growth and wanting everything to stay the same, is not going to foster the transformation God wants to do in your heart and life. God wants to take you higher, to bless you more, to help you become like Christ. Instead, embrace change, shift your eyes to Jesus, and step into what God asks or prompts you to do. Pray, "Lord, I look forward to You transforming my heart's desires to be pleasing to You. Search my heart and reveal to me what You want me to know and do to honor You, Lord. I invite You into my heart and say, 'Yes God,' to the change You want to create in me. I want to become all You designed me to be. Thank You for transforming my heart's desires to be pleasing to You. In Jesus's name, I pray. Amen."

5. ***Ignorance of God's Word and Lack of Time Seeking to Know God and Love God***
    When we don't spend time in prayer and study God's Word, we will be ignorant of who God is and what He wants to do in us. The truth sets you free only if you know the truth. Instead, carve out time every morning as you start your day to talk to God in prayer and to listen to God. One of the primary ways God speaks to us is through His Word. Read the Bible and ask God to reveal Himself to you. Here is an example: "Lord, thank You for blessing me with Your truth found in Your Word in the Bible. I come to You with an open heart, to know You more and love you more. Transform me into the person You designed me to be. Reveal to me what You want me to know,

say, and do per what you are teaching me. In Jesus's name, I pray. Amen." Write down what God is teaching you and the scripture verse that He reveals to you. God is a personal God and will give you revelation with a verse that speaks to whatever your need is.

You can navigate around these roadblocks. The Bible is your road map, and the Holy Spirit is your navigator. You can align to God's divine design, ignite your potential, and be all God designed you to be! Don't wait. Do it now!

Rules of the Road

1. *Use the road map, the Bible.* Read, study, and meditate on the Bible. All life's instructions are in the Bible. Seek to know and understand God's instructions.

2. *Fuel up daily.* Feed your Spirit with the Word of God every morning. Doing so will prevent you from running out of gas.

3. *Invite your navigator, guide, counselor, and advocate, the Holy Spirit, into your day to guide you.* You were not designed to know the way. God gives us the Holy Spirit to help us, equip us, and navigate for us.

4. *Slow down and make yourself available to be used by God to serve others.* Let others merge into your lane and stay unoffended. Know God wants to use you when He puts others in your path.

5. *Look out the windshield, not in the rearview mirror, to get to your destination and enjoy the ride.* There is a reason the windshield is larger than the rearview mirror. Let go of your mistakes, repent of any sins, and stay focused on where God is leading you.

6. *Get a weekly tune-up.* Take time every week to rest and worship our great God. This is essential for your engine to run smoothly and to be refreshed with God's perspective.

7. *You're in the driver's seat; turn on the ignition, step on the accelerator, take a leap of faith, and hand the wheel to Jesus!* This will ensure a successful trip.

Outline for Small-Group Bible Study

Week 1: Introductions
- Get to know one another.
- Icebreaker: describe a favorite gift you gave someone and what made it your favorite.
- Expectations: what to expect in this group and the group leader expectations.

Week 2: Milestone 1: Slow Down to Speed Up
- Read the chapter, complete your assessment, and discuss the results with your group.
- Discovery and application questions. Discuss as a group.

Week 3: Milestone 2: Discover Your Spiritual Gifts
- Read the chapter and discuss what you learned with your group.
- Discovery and application questions. Discuss as a group.

Week 4: Milestone 3: Develop Your Spiritual Gifts
- Read the chapter and discuss what you learned with your group.
- Take the spiritual gift assessment and share your spiritual gifts with one another.
- Discovery and application questions. Discuss as a group.

Week 5: Milestone 4: Discover and Align to God's Divine Design
- Finding Your Purpose

- Read the chapter and discuss what you learned with your group.
- Discovery and application questions. Discuss as a group.

Week 6: Milestone 5: Your Sweet Spot
- Ten Steps to Find Your Individual Purpose
- Read the chapter and discuss what you learned with your group.
- Complete your profile and action plan to serve. Share it with your group.
- Discovery and application questions. Discuss as a group.

Week 7: Appendix
- Review the options and select the ones that apply to you and your goals.

Options
- If you're a leader at your church, review the strategies for growth and discuss as a group.
- Review roadblocks and discuss how to navigate around them.
- Read the "Rules of the Road" and discuss them.
- Write out your testimony and share it with the group.
- Retake your assessment and discuss your progress since reading this book.

Sources

Milestone 1

- Findings in research done by George Barna, who found that a remarkable number of born-again Christians who have heard of spiritual gifts do not think they themselves have any spiritual gifts. In 1995, the percentage of born-again adults who did not think they had a spiritual gift was 4 percent. But by 2000 that number had risen to 21 percent! C. Peter Wagner, *Discover Your Spiritual Gifts*, Minneapolis, MN. Chosen, a division of Baker Publishing Group, 2002, 2005, 2012, page 39.
- Ray Johnston, Bayside Church senior pastor (*Outreach* magazine's fastest growing church in America in 2019), "87% of churches are stagnant or declining ..."
- *Merriam-Webster*, s.v. "Commit," accessed August 18, 2022, https://www.merriam-webster.com/dictionary/commit.
- Employees who are not engaged or who are actively disengaged cost the world $7.8 trillion in lost productivity, according to Gallup's State of the Global Workplace: 2022 Report. That's equal to 11 percent of global GDP. "State of the Global Workplace: 2022 Report," Gallup, accessed September 2022, https://www.gallup.com/workplace/349484/state-of-the-global-workplace.aspx.
- All scripture quotations, unless otherwise indicated, are taken from New International Version and New King James Version of Bible Gateway, accessed in September 2022.

"For I know the plans I have for you," declares the LORD, "plans to prosper you and not to harm you, plans to give you hope and a future." (Jeremiah 29:11 NIV)

For as in Adam all die, so in Christ all will be made alive. (1 Corinthians 15:22 NIV)

This is what the Lord says—he who made you, who formed you in the womb. (Isaiah 44:2a NIV)

- God designed everything in the world and spoke it into existence. Genesis 1 states that on the sixth day, God created man and made man in His image to be fruitful and multiply. "Then the LORD God formed a man from the dust of the ground and breathed into his nostrils the breath of life, and the man became a living being" (Genesis 2:7 NIV).
- In 1 Corinthians 12:1 (NIV), Paul writes, "Now about the gifts of the Spirit, brothers and sisters, I do not want you to be uninformed."

For from him and through him and for him are all things. To him be the glory forever! Amen. (Romans 11:36 NIV)

The LORD works out everything to its proper end. (Proverbs 16:4 NIV)

Those who look to him are radiant; their faces are never covered with shame. (Psalm 34:5 NIV)

Being confident of this, that he who began a good work in you will carry it on to completion until the day of Christ Jesus. (Philippians 1:6 NIV)

Milestone 2

Elect according to the foreknowledge of God the Father, through sanctification of the Spirit, unto obedience and sprinkling of the blood of Jesus Christ: Grace unto you, and peace, be multiplied. (1 Peter 1:2 NKJV)

For God so loved the world that he gave his one and only Son, that whoever believes in him shall not perish but have eternal life. (John 3:16 NIV)

Then he said to his disciples, "The harvest is plentiful, but the workers are few. Ask the Lord of the harvest, therefore, to send out workers into his harvest field." (Matthew 9:37–38 NIV)

They are not of the world, just as I am not of the world. Sanctify them by Your truth. Your word is truth. As You sent Me into the world, I also have sent them into the world. And for their sakes I sanctify Myself, that they also may be sanctified by the truth. (John 17:16–19 NKJV)

But as He who called you is holy, you also be holy in all your conduct, because it is written, "Be holy, for I am holy." (1 Peter 1:15–16 NKJV)

And be not conformed to this world: but be transformed by the renewing of your mind, that you may prove what is that good and acceptable and perfect will of God. (Romans 12:2 NKJV)

Saying, Father, if it is Your will, take this cup away from Me; nevertheless not My will, but Yours, be done. (Luke 22:42 NKJV)

"I am the vine; you are the branches. If you remain in me and I in you, you will bear much fruit; apart from me you can do nothing." (John 15:5 NIV)

"The Spirit of God has made me, And the breath of the Almighty gives me life." (Job 33:4 NKJV)

The proverbs of Solomon son of David, king of Israel: for gaining wisdom and instruction; for understanding words of insight. (Proverbs 1:1–2 NIV)

Who Himself bore our sins in His own body on the tree, that we, having died to sins, might live for righteousness— by whose stripes you were healed. (1 Peter 2:24 NKJV)

Create in me a clean heart, O God, And renew a steadfast spirit within me. (Psalm 51:10 NKJV)

How good and pleasant it is when God's people live together in unity! (Psalm 133:1 NIV)

That Christ may dwell in your hearts through faith; that you, being rooted and grounded in love. (Ephesians 3:17 NKJV)

After Job had prayed for his friends, the LORD restored his fortunes and gave him twice as much as he had before. (Job 42:10 NIV)

Submit yourselves, then, to God. Resist the devil, and he will flee from you. (James 4:7 NIV)

You, dear children, are from God and have overcome them, because the one who is in you is greater than the one who is in the world. (1 John 4:4 NIV)

Do not merely listen to the word, and so deceive yourselves. Do what it says. My intent is that you will be a doer of God's Word and will. (James 1:22 NIV)

Peter replied, "Repent and be baptized, every one of you, in the name of Jesus Christ for the forgiveness of your sins. And you will receive the gift of the Holy Spirit. The promise is for you and your children and for all who are far off—for all whom the Lord our God will call." (Acts 2:38–39 NIV)

But the natural man does not receive the things of the Spirit of God, for they are foolishness to him; nor can he know them, because they are spiritually discerned. (1 Corinthians 2:14 NKJV)

And you shall know the truth, and the truth shall make you free. (John 8:32 NKJV)

Pilate therefore said to Him, "Are You a king then?" Jesus answered, "You say rightly that I am a king. For this cause I was born, and for this cause I have come into the world, that I should bear witness to the truth. Everyone who is of the truth hears My voice." (John 18:37 NKJV)

Jesus answered, "I am the way and the truth and the life. No one comes to the Father except through me." (John 14:6 NIV)

These are the ones who were not defiled with women, for they are virgins. These are the ones who follow the Lamb wherever He goes. These were redeemed from among men, being firstfruits to God and to the Lamb. (Revelation 14:4 NKJV)

For the wages of sin is death, but the gift of God is eternal life in Christ Jesus our Lord. (Romans 6:23 NKJV)

Jesus answered, "Most assuredly, I say to you, unless one is born of water and the Spirit, he cannot enter the kingdom of God." (John 3:5 NKJV)

But you are not in the flesh but in the Spirit, if indeed the Spirit of God dwells in you. Now if anyone does not have the Spirit of Christ, he is not His. (Romans 8:9 NKJV)

But very truly I tell you, it is for your good that I am going away. Unless I go away, the Advocate will not come to you; but if I go, I will send him to you. (John 16:7 NIV)

Very truly I tell you, whoever believes in me will do the works I have been doing, and they will do even greater things than these, because I am going to the Father. (John 14:12 NIV)

Now to each one the manifestation of the Spirit is given for the common good. (1 Corinthians 12:7 NIV)

Once you were not a people, but now you are the people of God; once you had not received mercy, but now you have received mercy. (1 Peter 2:10 NIV)

- Romans 14:12 tells us that we will each give an account to God.

But the manifestation of the Spirit is given to each one for the profit of all. (Corinthians 12:7 NKJV)

Each of you should use whatever gift you have received to serve others, as faithful stewards of God's grace in its various forms. (1 Peter 4:10 NIV)

If anyone speaks, they should do so as one who speaks the very words of God. If anyone serves, they should do so with the strength God provides, so that in all things God may be praised through Jesus Christ. To him be the glory and the power for ever and ever. Amen. (1 Peter 4:11 NIV)

And be not conformed to this world: but be transformed by the renewing of your mind, that you may prove what is that good and acceptable and perfect will of God. (Romans 12:2 NKJV)

By faith Noah, when warned about things not yet seen, in holy fear built an ark to save his family. By his faith he condemned the world and became heir of the righteousness that is in keeping with faith. (Hebrews 11:7 NIV)

Now about the gifts of the Spirit, brothers and sisters, I do not want you to be uninformed. You know that when you were pagans, somehow or other you were influenced and led astray to mute idols. Therefore I want you to know that no one who is speaking by the Spirit of God says, "Jesus be cursed," and no one can say, "Jesus is Lord," except by the Holy Spirit. (1 Corinthians 12:1–3 NIV)

There are different kinds of gifts, but the same Spirit distributes them. There are different kinds of service, but the same Lord. There are different kinds of working, but in all of them and in everyone it is the same God at work. (1 Corinthians 12:4–6 NIV)

For God so loved the world that He gave His only begotten Son, that whoever believes in Him should not perish but have everlasting life. (John 3:16 NKJV)

- Romans 9:21, 23 tells us that we are vessels, containers. God is the fountain of life, as stated in John 1:4, which says that in Him, the one who is in the Word and God Himself, there is life. Life is in Him, so He is the tree of life.

Jesus went through all the towns and villages, teaching in their synagogues, proclaiming the good news of the kingdom and healing every disease and sickness. When he saw the crowds, he had compassion on them, because they were harassed and helpless, like sheep without a shepherd. Then he said to his disciples, "The harvest is plentiful but the workers are few. Ask the Lord of the harvest, therefore, to send out workers into his harvest field." (Matthew 9:35–38 NIV)

Therefore, since Christ suffered in his body, arm yourselves also with the same attitude, because whoever suffers in the body is done with sin. As a result, they do not live the rest of their earthly lives for evil human desires, but rather for the will of God. For you have spent enough time in the past doing what pagans choose to do—living in debauchery, lust, drunkenness, orgies, carousing and detestable idolatry. They are surprised that you do not join them in their reckless, wild living, and they heap abuse on you. But they will have to give account to him who is ready to judge the living and the dead. For this is the reason the gospel was preached even to those who are now dead, so that they might be judged according to human standards in regard to the body, but live according to God in regard to the spirit. The end of all things is near. Therefore be alert and of sober mind so that you may pray. Above all, love each other deeply, because love covers over a multitude of sins. Offer hospitality to one another without grumbling. Each of you should use whatever gift you have received to serve others, as faithful stewards of God's grace in its various forms. If anyone speaks, they should do so as one who speaks the very words of God. If anyone serves, they should do so with the strength God provides, so that in all things God may be praised through Jesus Christ. To him be the glory and the power for ever and ever. Amen. (1 Peter 4–11 NIV)

Many are the plans in a person's heart, but it is the Lord's purpose that prevails. (Proverbs 19:21 NIV)

For I have come down from heaven not to do my will but to do the will of him who sent me. (John 6:38 NIV)

"For my thoughts are not your thoughts, neither are your ways my ways," declares the LORD. "As the heavens are higher than the earth, so are my ways higher than your ways and my thoughts than your thoughts." (Isaiah 55:8–9 NIV)

For by the grace given me I say to every one of you: Do not think of yourself more highly than you ought, but rather think of yourself with sober judgment, in accordance with the faith God has distributed to each of you. For just as each of us has one body with many members, and these members do not all have the same function, so in Christ we, though many, form one body, and each member belongs to all the others. We have different gifts, according to the grace given to each of us. If your gift is prophesying, then prophesy in accordance with your faith; if it is serving, then serve; if it is teaching, then teach; if it is to encourage, then give encouragement; if it is giving, then give generously; if it is to lead, do it diligently; if it is to show mercy, do it cheerfully. (Romans 12:3–8 NIV)

Follow the way of love and eagerly desire the gifts of the Spirit, especially prophecy. (1 Corinthians 14:1 NIV)

But he who prophesies speaks to the people for their strengthening, encouraging and comfort. (1 Corinthians 14:3 NIV)

For you, brethren, have been called to liberty; only do not use liberty as an opportunity for the flesh, but through love serve one another. (Galatians 5:13 NKJV)

For this reason I have sent Timothy to you, who is my beloved and faithful son in the Lord, who will remind you of my ways in Christ, as I teach everywhere in every church. (Corinthians 4:17 NKJV)

Beware, brethren, lest there be in any of you an evil heart of unbelief in departing from the living God; but exhort one another daily, while it is called "Today," lest any of you be hardened through the deceitfulness of sin. (Hebrews 3:12–13 NKJV)

Give, and it will be given to you: good measure, pressed down, shaken together, and running over will be put into your bosom. For with the same measure that you use, it will be measured back to you. (Luke 6:38 NKJV)

A bishop then must be blameless, the husband of one wife, temperate, sober-minded, of good behavior, hospitable, able to teach. (1 Timothy 3:2 NKJV)

Therefore, as the elect of God, holy and beloved, put on tender mercies, kindness, humility, meekness, longsuffering. (Colossians 3:12 NKJV)

And He Himself gave some to be apostles, some prophets, some evangelists, and some pastors and teachers. (Ephesians 4:11 NKJV)

"Do not neglect the gift that is in you, which was given to you by prophecy with the laying on of the hands of the eldership." (1 Timothy 4:14 NKJV)

Now about the gifts of the Spirit, brothers and sisters, I do not want you to be uninformed. You know that when you were pagans, somehow or other you were influenced and led astray to mute idols. Therefore I want you to know that no one who is speaking by the Spirit of God says, "Jesus be cursed," and no one can say, "Jesus is Lord," except by the Holy Spirit. (1 Corinthians 12:1–3 NIV)

There are different kinds of gifts, but the same Spirit distributes them. There are different kinds of service, but the same Lord. There are different kinds of working, but in all of them and in everyone it is the same God at work. (1 Corinthians 12:4–6 NIV)

Now to each one the manifestation of the Spirit is given for the common good. To one there is given through the Spirit a message of wisdom, to another a message of knowledge by means of the same Spirit, to another faith by the same Spirit, to another gifts of healing by that one Spirit, to another miraculous powers, to another prophecy, to another distinguishing between spirits, to another speaking in different kinds of tongues, and to still another the interpretation of tongues. All these are the work of one and the same Spirit, and he distributes them to each one, just as he determines. (1 Corinthians 12:1–7 NIV)

To one there is given through the Spirit a message of wisdom, to another a message of knowledge by means of the same Spirit, to another faith by the same Spirit, to another gifts of healing by that one Spirit, to another miraculous powers, to another prophecy, to another distinguishing between spirits, to another speaking in different kinds of tongues, and to still another the interpretation of tongues. (1 Corinthians 12: 8–10 NIV)

But the Helper, the Holy Spirit, whom the Father will send in My name, He will teach you all things, and bring to your remembrance all things that I said to you. (John 14:26 NKJV)

How good and pleasant it is when God's people live together in unity! (Psalm 133:1 NIV)

As a prisoner for the Lord, then, I urge you to live a life worthy of the calling you have received. Be completely humble and gentle; be patient, bearing with one another in love. Make every effort to keep the unity of the Spirit through the bond of peace. (Ephesians 4:1–3 NIV)

But the manifestation of the Spirit is given to each one for the profit of all. (1 Corinthians 12:7 NKJV)

And the same is true for you. Since you are so eager to have the special abilities the Spirit gives, seek those that will strengthen the whole church. (1 Corinthians 14:12 NLT)

To equip his people for works of service, so that the body of Christ may be built up. (Ephesians 4:12 NIV)

Finally, brothers and sisters, whatever is true, whatever is noble, whatever is right, whatever is pure, whatever is lovely, whatever is admirable—if anything is excellent or praiseworthy—think about such things. (Philippians 4:8 NIV)

And He Himself gave some to be apostles, some prophets, some evangelists, and some pastors and teachers, for the equipping of the saints for the work of ministry, for the edifying of the body of Christ, till we all come to the unity of the faith and of the knowledge of the Son of God, to a perfect man, to the measure of the stature of the fullness of Christ. (Ephesians 4:11–13 NKJV)

Now hope does not disappoint, because the love of God has been poured out in our hearts by the Holy Spirit who was given to us. (Romans 5:5 NKJV)

For God so loved the world that He gave His only begotten Son, that whoever believes in Him should not perish but have everlasting life. (John 3:16 NKJV)

Then Jesus spoke to them again, saying, "I am the light of the world. He who follows Me shall not walk in darkness, but have the light of life." (John 8:12 NKJV)

So it is with you. Since you are eager for gifts of the Spirit, try to excel in those that build up the church. (1 Corinthians 14:12 NIV)

To equip his people for works of service, so that the body of Christ may be built up. (Ephesians 4:12 NIV)

But the manifestation of the Spirit is given to each one for the profit of all. (1 Corinthians 2:7 NKJV)

Each of you should use whatever gift you have received to serve others, as faithful stewards of God's grace in its various forms. (1 Peter 4:10 NIV)

If anyone speaks, they should do so as one who speaks the very words of God. If anyone serves, they should do so with the strength God provides, so that in all things God may be praised through Jesus Christ. To him be the glory and the power for ever and ever. Amen. (1 Peter 4:11 NIV)

That you were enriched in everything by Him in all utterance and all knowledge, even as the testimony of Christ was confirmed in you, so that you come short in no gift, eagerly waiting for the revelation of our Lord Jesus Christ. (1 Corinthians 1:5–7 NKJV)

"But you will receive power when the Holy Spirit comes on you; and you will be my witnesses in Jerusalem, and in all Judea and Samaria, and to the ends of the earth." (Acts 1:8 NIV)

The Great Commission: Then Jesus came to them and said, "All authority in heaven and on earth has been given to me. Therefore go and make disciples of all nations, baptizing them in the name of the Father and of the Son and of the Holy Spirit, and teaching them to obey everything

I have commanded you. And surely I am with you always, to the very end of the age." (Matthew 28:18–20 NIV)

The Great Commandment: Jesus replied: "'Love the Lord your God with all your heart and with all your soul and with all your mind.' This is the first and greatest commandment. And the second is like it: 'Love your neighbor as yourself.' All the Law and the Prophets hang on these two commandments." (Matthew 22: 37–40 NIV)

- *Merriam-Webster*, s.v. "Commit," accessed August 18, 2022, https://www.merriam-webster.com/dictionary/commit.

Those who accepted his message were baptized, and about three thousand were added to their number that day. They devoted themselves to the apostles' teaching and to fellowship, to the breaking of bread and to prayer. Every day they continued to meet together in the temple courts. They broke bread in their homes and ate together with glad and sincere hearts. (Acts 2:41–42, 46 NIV)

And do not present your members as instruments of unrighteousness to sin, but present yourselves to God as being alive from the dead, and your members as instruments of righteousness to God. (Romans 6:13 NKJV)

"You are the light of the world. A town built on a hill cannot be hidden. Neither do people light a lamp and put it under a bowl. Instead they put it on its stand, and it gives light to everyone in the house. In the same way, let your light shine before others, that they may see your good deeds and glorify your Father in heaven." (Matthew 5:14–16 NIV)

Therefore let us move beyond the elementary teachings about Christ and be taken forward to maturity. (Hebrews 6:1 NIV)

In fact, though by this time you ought to be teachers, you need someone to teach you the elementary truths of

God's word all over again. You need milk, not solid food! (Hebrews 5:12 NIV)

"As each one has received a gift, minister it to one another, as good stewards of the manifold grace of God." (1 Peter 4:10 NKJV)

- Ephesians 4:11–12 (NIV) tells us, "So Christ himself gave the apostles, the prophets, the evangelists, the pastors and teachers, to equip his people for the works of service so that the body of Christ may be built up." Each of us has gifts that can be of service inside the church.

Therefore, I urge you, brothers and sisters, in view of God's mercy, to offer your bodies as a living sacrifice, holy and pleasing to God—this is your true and proper worship. Do not conform to the pattern of this world, but be transformed by the renewing of your mind. Then you will be able to test and approve what God's will is—his good, pleasing and perfect will. (Romans 12:1–2 NIV)

- As stated by Sylvia Gaston in the November 13, 2021, article "Life Notes: Testify to the times you have seen God's work" in the *Sentinel*. "The word testimony in Hebrew is 'Aydooth' which means 'do it again with the same power and authority.' Every time we speak out, or read a testimony, we are saying 'Lord, do it again with the same power and authority.'" https://hanfordsentinel.com/lifestyles/faith-and-values/religion/life-notes-testify-to-the-times-you-have-seen-gods-work/article_93b900a3-c0b8-5c20-b549-fc72707d6bb3.html#:~:text=The%20word%20testimony%20in%20Hebrew,the%20same%20power%20and%20authority.
- Not only is religion growing overall, but Christianity specifically is growing. With a 1.17 percent growth rate, almost 2.56 billion people will identify as a Christian by the middle of 2022. By 2050, that number is expected to top 3.33 billion. From page 66 of *7 Encouraging Trends of Global Christianity in 2022,*

Lifeway Research, December 5, 2022, https://research. lifeway.com/2022/01/31/7-encouraging-trends-of-global-christianity-in-2022/.

Milestone 4

Being confident of this, that he who began a good work in you will carry it on to completion until the day of Christ Jesus. (Philippians 1:6 NIV)

But be doers of the word, and not hearers only, deceiving yourselves. For if anyone is a hearer of the word and not a doer, he is like a man observing his natural face in a mirror; for he observes himself, goes away, and immediately forgets what kind of man he was. But he who looks into the perfect law of liberty and continues in it, and is not a forgetful hearer but a doer of the work, this one will be blessed in what he does. (James 1: 22–25 NKJV)

- I like what Dr. David Jeremiah wrote in his *Turning Points Magazine & Devotional*, dated November 2021: "A Biblical View of Purpose referencing the Bible and Ken Boa's three tiered paradigm for talking about man's purpose: the ultimate purpose, universal purpose, and unique purpose of man.

Dr. David Jeremiah goes on to stay, "I'm going to use Boa's three-fold outline to jumpstart my own take on purpose, specifically how we can discover our purpose in Scriptures.[1]"

Below is a summary of what I learned.

Tier one is our permanent purpose, tier two is our progressive purpose, and tier three is our personal purpose."

1: Permanent Purpose

- "Then I saw a new heaven and a new earth, for the first heaven and the first earth had passed away, and there was no longer any sea (Revelation 21:1 NIV).
- Our permanent purpose is to spend eternity with God. The world is not our home. Our first purpose with the gift of salvation is to spend eternity with God.

2: Progressive Purpose

- Dr. David Jeremiah goes on to say, "But for the moment, we are here on earth, making progress toward our permanent purpose. God is gathering to Himself all those who dwell with Him for eternity. And that gathering place is called, the Church-the Body of Christ. (1 Corinthians 12–27; Ephesians 4:12). Paul makes it clear that our progressive purpose is to be a member, a participant in building up the Body of Christ. But our progressive purpose goes even deeper. God's progressive purpose in your life and mine is for us to be conformed to the image of Christ. Paul makes it clear in 1 Corinthians 12-14, that our progressive purpose is to be a member, a participant, in the building up of the Body of Christ."

"And we know that in all things God works for the good of those who love him, who have been called according to his purpose. For those God foreknew he also predestined to be conformed to the image of his Son, that he might be the firstborn among many brothers and sisters" (Romans 8:28–29 NIV).

To equip his people for works of service, so that the body of Christ may be built up (Ephesians 4:12 NIV).

3: Personal Purpose

- Dr. David Jeremiah says our personal purpose is to "glorify God and enjoy Him forever."

The Great Commandment: Jesus replied: "'Love the Lord your God with all your heart and with all your soul and with all your mind.' This is the first and greatest commandment. And the second is like it: 'Love your neighbor as yourself.' All the Law and the Prophets hang on these two commandments." (Matthew 22:37–40 NIV)

The Great Commission: Jesus said, "All authority in heaven and on earth has been given to me. Therefore, go and make disciples of all nations, baptizing them in the name of the Father and the Son and the Holy Spirit, and teaching them to obey everything I have commanded you. And surely I am with you always to the very end of the age." (Matthew 28:18–20 NIV)

For God so loved the world that he gave his one and only Son, that whoever believes in him shall not perish but have eternal life. (John 3:16 NIV)

- In *The Purpose Driven Life*, Pastor Rick Warren suggests that these purposes are worship, fellowship, discipleship, ministry, and witnessing and that they are derived from the Great Commandment (Matthew 22:37–40) and the Great Commission (Matthew 28:19–20). Pastor Rick Warren writes that every church is driven by something. To understand each purpose fully, I recommend you read his book.

"For My thoughts are not your thoughts, Nor are your ways My ways," says the LORD.

"For as the heavens are higher than the earth,
So are My ways higher than your ways,
And My thoughts than your thoughts."
(Isaiah 55:8–9 NKJV)

Noah did everything just as God commanded him. (Genesis 6:22 NIV)

So then faith comes from hearing, and hearing by the word of God. (Romans 10:17 NKJV)

"And teaching them to obey everything I have commanded you. And surely I am with you always, to the very end of the age." (Matthew 28:20 NIV)

For though by this time you ought to be teachers, you need someone to teach you again the first principles of the oracles of God; and you have come to need milk and not solid food. (Hebrews 5:12 NKJV)

Those who accepted his message were baptized, and about three thousand were added to their number that day. They devoted themselves to the apostles' teaching and to fellowship, to the breaking of bread and to prayer. Everyone was filled with awe at the many wonders and signs performed by the apostles. All the believers were together and had everything in common. They sold property and possessions to give to anyone who had need. Every day they continued to meet together in the temple courts. They broke bread in their homes and ate together with glad and sincere hearts, praising God and enjoying the favor of all the people. And the Lord added to their number daily those who were being saved. (Acts 2:41–47 NIV)

For we are God's handiwork, created in Christ Jesus to do good works, which God prepared in advance for us to do. (Ephesians 2:10 NIV)

Therefore go and make disciples of all nations, baptizing them in the name of the Father and of the Son and of the Holy Spirit. (Matthew 28:19 NIV)

We are therefore Christ's ambassadors, as though God were making his appeal through us. We implore you on Christ's behalf: Be reconciled to God. (2 Corinthians 5:20 NIV)

For as we have many members in one body, but all the members do not have the same function, so we, being many, are one body in Christ, and individually members of one another. Having then gifts differing according to the grace that is given to us, let us use them: if prophecy, let us prophesy in proportion to our faith. (Romans 12:4–6 NKJV)

Guard your heart, for it is the wellspring of life. (Proverbs 4:23 NIV)

"So I say to you: Ask and it will be given to you; seek and you will find; knock and the door will be opened to you." (Luke 11:9 NIV)

For we are His workmanship, created in Christ Jesus for good works, which God prepared beforehand that we should walk in them. (Ephesians 2:10 NKJV)

And now, compelled by the Spirit, I am going to Jerusalem, not knowing what will happen to me there. (Acts 20:22 NIV)

We have different gifts, according to the grace given to each of us. If your gift is prophesying, then prophesy in accordance with your faith. (Romans 12:6a NIV)

Have you experienced so much in vain—if it really was in vain? (Galatians 3:4 NIV)

This is a trustworthy saying. And I want you to stress these things, so that those who have trusted in God may be careful to devote themselves to doing what is good. These things are excellent and profitable for everyone. (Titus 3:8 NIV)

For we are His workmanship, created in Christ Jesus for good works, which God prepared beforehand that we should walk in them. (Ephesians 2:10 NKJV)

Equip you with everything good for doing his will, and may he work in us what is pleasing to him, through Jesus Christ, to whom be glory for ever and ever. Amen. (Hebrews 13:21 NIV)

And there are diversities of activities, but it is the same God who works all in all. (1 Corinthians 12:6 NKJV)

For the gifts and the calling of God are irrevocable. (Romans 11:29 NKJV)

- Your destiny, as defined by Pastor Tony Evans, is your customized life calling for which God has equipped and ordained you in order to bring Him the greatest glory and maximum expansion of His kingdom. Pastor Tony Evans, "Dr. Tony Evans's Quotes on Discovering your Destiny," Kingdom Grace Media, last modified September 25, 2021, https://kingdomgracemedia.medium.com/dr-tony-evanss-quotes-on-discovering-your-destiny-feecba01a0.

And if you have not been trustworthy with someone else's property, who will give you property of your own? (Luke 16:12 NIV)

But God has revealed them to us through His Spirit. For the Spirit searches all things, yes, the deep things of God. For what man knows the things of a man except the spirit of the man which is in him? Even so no one knows the things of God except the Spirit of God. Now we have received, not the spirit of the world, but the Spirit who is from God, that we might know the things that have been freely given to us by God. (1 Corinthians 2:10–12 NKJV)

For you created my inmost being; you knit me together in my mother's womb. I praise you because I am fearfully and wonderfully made; your works are wonderful, I know that full well. My frame was not hidden from you when I was made in the secret place, when I was woven together in the depths of the earth. Your eyes saw my unformed body; all the days ordained for me were written in your book before one of them came to be. (Psalm 139:13–16 NIV)

Before I formed you in the womb I knew you, before you were born I set you apart; I appointed you as a prophet to the nations. (Jeremiah 1:5 NIV)

And I thank Christ Jesus our Lord who has enabled me, because He counted me faithful, putting me into the ministry. (1 Timothy 1:12 NKJV)

The one who calls you is faithful, and he will do it. (1 Thessalonians 5:24 NIV)

I press toward the goal for the prize of the upward call of God in Christ Jesus. (Philippians 3:14 NKJV)

He told them another parable: "The kingdom of heaven is like a mustard seed, which a man took and planted in his field. Though it is the smallest of all seeds, yet when it grows, it is the largest of garden plants and becomes a tree, so that the birds come and perch in its branches." (Matthew 13:31–32 NIV)

- Pastor Wayne Cordeiro, *Dream Releasers* (Ventura, CA: Gospel Light Worldwide, 2002), 27.

Now that you know these things, you will be blessed if you do them. (John 13:17 NIV)

For I know the thoughts that I think toward you, says the LORD, thoughts of peace and not of evil, to give you a future and a hope. (Jeremiah 29:11 NKJV)

- Jim Collins, *Good to Great: Why Some Companies Make the Leap and Others Don't* (New York: HarperBusiness, 2001), 87.

Roadblocks

When I am afraid, I put my trust in you. (Psalm 56:3 NIV)

Susan A. Lund Biography

Susan A. Lund is a sales, leadership, and productivity expert. She is the president of MR3, a metrics-driven sales, leadership, and productivity consulting and training firm. Susan has over thirty years of experience in business, sales, leadership, training, and coaching thousands of individuals, teams, and organizations to ignite their potential and grow.

Susan has a heart for God, helping people succeed and igniting their potential. Millions of believers don't know their spiritual gifts, purpose, or God's divine design for their life. Unfortunately, they have unwrapped gifts and unrealized dreams and are extinguishing their God-given potential. As a result, they are missing out on living in the power and presence of God's amazing design for their life.

God has used Susan to inspire, equip, and empower hundreds of people to grow in their relationships with Him, gain clarity of their purpose, ignite their potential, and align to God's divine design for their life. When they do, they experience great joy, and God's church grows!

Susan gives God credit for all her success and acknowledges that every good thing that flows through her comes from God. She believes God designed us to align to His divine design, to ignite our God-given potential and be all God designed us to be.

Susan is the author of three books: *Ignite Your Selling Potential, 7 Simple Accelerators to Drive Revenue and Results Fast*; *Prayer Journal for Growth*; and *Ignite Your Potential: A Road Map to Discover Your Spiritual Gifts, Find Your Purpose, and Align to God's Divine Design.*

She is also a professional speaker who loves to speak to leadership teams, the next generation, young adults, and groups on practical strategies and steps to ignite their potential and grow.

In her free time, Susan enjoys spending time with her family, being outdoors, and giving back to the community.